MARISOL

BY JOSÉ RIVERA

DRAMATISTS
PLAY SERVICE
INC.

For Heather and Adena

MARISOL was produced by The New York Shakespeare Festival (George C. Wolfe, Producer), in association with The Hartford Stage Company (Mark Lamos, Artistic Director), in New York City, in May, 1993. It was directed by Michael Greif; the set design was by Debra Booth; the costume design was by Angela Wendt; the lighting design was by Kenneth Posner; the sound design was by David Budries; the violence director was David Leong; the original music was by Jill Jaffe and the production stage manager was Lori M. Doyle. The cast was as follows:

ANGEL .... Danitra Vance
MARISOL .... Cordelia González
YOUNG WOMAN .... Doris Difarnecio
MAN WITH GOLF CLUB, MAN WITH
   ICE CREAM, LENNY, MAN WITH
   SCAR TISSUE .... Skipp Sudduth
JUNE .... Anne O'Sullivan
WOMAN WITH FURS,
   RADIO ANNOUNCER .... Phyllis Somerville
VOICES, HOMELESS PEOPLE .... Doris Difarnecio,
                 Decater James, Robert Jimenez,
              Anne O'Sullivan, Phyllis Somerville
GUITARIST .... Chris Cunningham

MARISOL was produced by The Hartford Stage Company, in Hartford, Connecticut, in March, 1993. It was directed by Michael Greif; the set design was by Debra Booth; the costume design was by Gabriel Berry; the lighting design was by Kenneth Posner; the sound design was by David Budries; the violence director was David Leong and the production stage manager was Barbara Reo. The cast was as follows:

ANGEL .... Danitra Vance
MARISOL .... Cordelia González
YOUNG WOMAN .... Doris Difarnecio
MAN WITH GOLF CLUB, MAN WITH
   ICE CREAM, LENNY, MAN WITH
   SCAR TISSUE .... Skipp Sudduth

JUNE .... Anne O'Sullivan
WOMAN WITH FURS,
    RADIO ANNOUNCER .... Phyllis Somerville
VOICES, HOMELESS PEOPLE .... Doris Difarnecio,
                        Decater James, Anne O'Sullivan,
                                    Phyllis Somerville

MARISOL was produced by La Jolla Playhouse (Des McAnuff, Artistic Director), in La Jolla, California, on September 8, 1992. It was directed by Tina Landau; the set design was by Robert Brill; the costume design was by Janice Benning; the lighting design was by John Martin and the sound design and original music was by John Gromada. The cast was as follows:

ANGEL .... Esther Scott
MARISOL .... Cordelia González
YOUNG WOMAN .... Micha Espinosa
MAN WITH GOLF CLUB .... David Fenner
MAN WITH ICE CREAM .... Robert A. Owens
LENNY .... Michael Harris
MAN WITH SCAR TISSUE,
    RADIO ANNOUNCER .... Joseph Urla
JUNE .... Susan Berman
WOMAN WITH FURS .... Amy Scholl
VOICES, HOMELESS PEOPLE .... Micha Espinosa,
                        David Fenner, Robert A. Owens,
                                    Amy Scholl, Joseph Urla

MARISOL received its world premiere at the 1992 Annual Humana Festival of New American Plays at the Actors Theatre of Louisville (Jon Jory, Producing Director), in Louisville, Kentucky, on March 13, 1992. It was directed by Marcus Stern; the set design was by Paul Owen; the costume design was by Laura A. Patterson; the lighting design was by Mary Louise Geiger; the sound design was by Darron West and the stage manager was James Mountcastle. The cast was as follows:

MARISOL was originally commissioned and developed by INTAR Hispanic American Arts Center (Max Ferra, Artistic Director) through a grant from the Rockefeller Foundation.

Special thanks to Heather Dundas, Anne O'Sullivan, Mel Kenyon, Max Stafford-Clark, Mame Hunt, Roberta Levitow, Morgan Jenness, Tanya Berezin, Adrienne Heigel, Circle Rep's Playwrights Lab, Max Ferra, Robin Miles, Cordelia González, Wiley Hausam, Scott Renderer, Sheila Dabney, David Chandler, Bill Cwikowski, Elizabeth Clemens, Monique Cintron, Bill Quiggley, Benjamin Lloyd, Leslie Hope, Peter Sagal, Roxanne Rogers, Bill Pullman, Charles Stratton, Roxanne Biggs, Alison Taylor and, the staff, cast, crew, designers and director of the Actors Theatre of Louisville.

CHARACTERS

MARISOL, a Puerto Rican woman, 26
ANGEL, Marisol's guardian angel, a young black woman
SUBWAY ANNOUNCER
MAN WITH GOLF CLUB
1ST VOICE
2ND VOICE
3RD VOICE
JUNE, Marisol's friend, Irish-American, 36
RADIO VOICE
MAN WITH ICE CREAM
LENNY, June's brother, 34
WOMAN WITH FURS
MAN WITH SCAR TISSUE
HOMELESS PEOPLE

CAST BREAKDOWN

Actor 1. Marisol
Actor 2. June, 2nd Voice
Actor 3. Angel
Actor 4. 1st Voice, Woman With Furs, Homeless Person
Actor 5. Subway Announcer, Man With Golf Club,
        3rd Voice, Radio Voice, Man With Ice Cream,
        Lenny, Man With Scar Tissue

TIME AND PLACE

New York City. The present. Winter.

MARISOL

ACT ONE

Scene 1

New York City. The present.

Lights up on an upstage brick wall running the width of the stage and going as high as the theatre will allow. The windows in the wall are shielded by iron security gates. The highest windows are boarded up.

Spray-painted on the wall is this graffiti-poem:
"The moon carries the souls of dead people to heaven.
The new moon is dark and empty.
It fills up every month
with new glowing souls
then it carries its silent burden to God. WAKE UP."

The "WAKE UP" looks like it was added to the poem by someone else.

Downstage of the wall is a tall ladder coming down at an angle. Sitting on the ladder is Marisol's Guardian Angel.

The Angel is a young, black woman in ripped jeans, sneakers and black T-shirt. Crude silver wings hang limply from the back of the Angel's diamond-studded black leather jacket. Though she radiates tremendous heat and light, there's something tired and lonely about the Angel: she looks like an urban warrior, a suffering, burnt-out soldier of some lost cause. She

9

watches the scene below with intense concern.

Floating in the sky is a small gold crown inside a clear glass box.

Lights up on the subway car: a filth-covered bench.

It's late night. Late winter.

Marisol Perez, an attractive Puerto Rican woman of 26, sits in the subway car. Marisol has dark hair and deep, smart, dark eyes. She is a young urban professional: smartly dressed, reading the New York Times, *returning to her Bronx apartment after a long day at her Manhattan job. She wears heavy winter clothing. She has no idea she's being watched by an angel.*

SUBWAY ANNOUNCER. ... and a pleasant evening to all the ladies. 180th Street will be the next and last stop. Step lively, guard your valuables, trust no one. *(The Man With Golf Club enters the subway car. He's a young white man, 20s, in a filthy black T-shirt and ripped jeans; his long matted hair hangs over blazing eyes. His shoes are rags and his mind is shot. The Man looks at Marisol and "shoots" the club like an Uzi. Marisol has taught herself not to show fear or curiosity on the subway. She digs deeper into her paper. The Man talks to Marisol.)*
GOLF CLUB. It was the shock that got me. I was so shocked all I could see was pain all around me: little spinning starlights of pain 'cause of the shocking thing the angel just told me. *(He waits for a reaction. Marisol refuses to look at him.)* You see, she was always *there* for me. I could *count* on her. She was my very own God-blessed little angel! My own gift from God! *(No response. He makes a move toward Marisol. She looks at him, quickly sizing him up ...)*
MARISOL. God help you, you get in my face.
GOLF CLUB. But last night she crawled into the box I occupy on 180th Street in the Bronx. I was sleeping: nothing special

walking through my thoughts 'cept the usual panic over my empty stomach, and the windchill factor, and how, oh *how*, was I *ever* gonna replace my lost Citibank MasterCard?

MARISOL.   I have no money. *(Marisol tries to slide away from the Man, trying to show no fear. He follows.)*

GOLF CLUB.   She folded her hot silver angel wings under her leather jacket and creeped into my box last night, reordering the air, waking me up with the shock, the bad news that she was gonna *leave me forever ...*

MARISOL.   *(Getting freaked.)* Man, why don't you just get a job?!

GOLF CLUB.   *Don't you see?* She once stopped Nazi skinheads from setting me on fire in Van Cortlandt Park! Do you get it now, lady?! I live on the street! I am dead meat without my guardian angel! I'm gonna be *food* ... a fucking *appetizer* for all the Hitler youth and their cans of *gasoline ...* *(The Man lunges at Marisol and rips the newspaper from her. She's on her feet, ready for a fight.)*

MARISOL.   *(To God.)* Okay, God! Kill him now! Take him out!

GOLF CLUB.   *(Truly worried.)* That means you don't have any protection either. Your guardian angel is gonna leave you too. That means, in the next *four or five seconds,* I could change the entire course of your life ...

MARISOL.   *(To God.)* Blast him into little bits! Turn him into salt!

GOLF CLUB.   *(Calm, almost pitying.)* I could turn you into one of me. I could fix it so every time you look in the mirror ... every time you dream ... or close your eyes in some hopeless logic that closed eyes are a shield against nightmares ... *you're gonna think you turned into me ...* *(The Man makes a move toward Marisol. The Angel reacts. There's an earsplitting scream as the subway stops. Marisol and the Man are thrown violently across the subway car. The Man falls. Marisol seizes her chance, pushes the disoriented Man away, and runs out of the subway car into the street. Lights to black on the subway. The Man exits in the dark.)*

Scene 2

Lights up on the street: a small empty space with a battered city trash can. It's snowing lightly. The shivering Marisol stops to look up at the sky. She crosses herself.

MARISOL. Thank you. *(No response from the Angel. It stops snowing as Marisol leaves the street and enters:)*

Scene 3

Lights up on Marisol's apartment: bed, table, lamp, clock, off-stage bathroom and large romanticized picture of a traditional Catholic guardian angel on the wall.

Marisol quickly runs in, slamming and locking the door behind her. She runs to the window to make sure the security gates are locked.

She tries to catch her breath. She takes off her coat. She notices an army of cockroaches on the floor. She stomps them angrily until every last one is dead. This seems to make her feel a little better.

She collapses into bed. She pounds her pillow angrily. Exhausted, she checks a knife she keeps under her pillow. She puts it back and lies on her bed, trying to calm herself and just breathe.

As she changes her clothes she fixes herself a drink and downs it.

She checks the crucifix, horseshoe, rabbit's foot, prayer cards, milagros, *medicine bundles, statuettes of Buddha and other good-luck charms kept under the bed. She crosses herself and closes her eyes.*

MARISOL. Matthew, Mark, Luke and John. Bless the bed that I lie on. Four corners to my bed. Four angels 'round my head. One to watch and one to pray. And two to bear my soul away. *(Marisol crosses herself, opens her eyes, and lies down. Then the noises begin. They come at Marisol from apartments all around her. Doors are slammed, bottles smashed, radiator pipes pounded, stereos played loud. Then the Voices join in.)*

1ST VOICE. *(Female.) Ave Maria purisima, donde esta el* heat? *(Marisol sits up. She can't believe this bullshit is starting again ...)*

2ND VOICE. *(Female, a high-decibel shriek.)* Matthew? It's Sandy! I KNOW YOU'RE IN THERE. STOP HIDING FROM ME, YOU MALIGNANT FUCK! *(Marisol starts rubbing her pounding head.)*

3RD VOICE. *(Male.)* Ah yeah yeah man you gotta help me man they broke my fuckin' *head* open ... *(Marisol runs to her window, shakes the iron gates.)*

MARISOL. *Mira,* people are trying to sleep!

2ND VOICE. YOU'RE PISSING ME OFF, MATTHEW, OPEN THE DOOR!

1ST VOICE. *Donde esta el* heat?? *NO TENGO* HEAT, *COÑO!*

2ND VOICE. MATTHEEEEEEEEEEEEEEEEEW! *(Marisol dives back into bed, covering her head, trying not to hear. The noises increase and the Voices come faster, louder, overlapping ...)*

3RD VOICE. ... I was jus' tryin' to sell 'em some dope man ...

2ND VOICE. MATTHEW, GODDAMNIT, IT'S SANDY! SANDY! YOUR *GIRLFRIEND,* YOU WITLESS *COCK!*

1ST VOICE. *Me vas a matar* without *el* fucking heat!!

2ND VOICE. MATTHEEEEEEEEWWWWWWW! OPEN THIS DOOOOOOOOOOOOOR!

3RD VOICE. ... so they hadda go bust my fuckin' head open oh look haha there go my busted brains floppin' 'round the floor

I'm gonna step right on 'em I'm not careful man I shouldda got their fuckin' *badge* numbers ... *(Marisol bangs on the floor with a shoe.)*

MARISOL. Some people work in the morning!!

3RD VOICE. ... think I'll pick up my brains right now man get a shovel 'n' scoop up my soakin' brainbag off this messy linoleum floor man sponge up my absentee motherfuckin' *mind* ...

2ND VOICE. THAT'S IT, MATTHEW! YOU'RE DEAD. I'M COMING BACK WITH A GUN AND I'M GONNA KILL YOU AND THEN I'M GONNA KILL EVERYONE IN THIS APART-MENT BUILDING INCLUDING THE CHILDREN! *(The Voices stop. Marisol waits. Thinking it's over, Marisol gets into bed and tries to sleep. Beat. Marisol starts to nod off. There's suddenly furious knocking at Marisol's door.)* MATTHEW! I'M BACK! I'VE GOT MY DADDY'S GUN! AND YOU'RE GONNA DIE RIGHT NOW! *(Marisol runs to the door.)*

MARISOL. Matthew doesn't live here! You have the wrong apartment!

2ND VOICE. Matthew, *who's that???*

MARISOL. Matthew lives next door!!

2ND VOICE. IS THAT YOUR NEW GIRLFRIEND, MATTHEW???! OH YOU'RE DEAD. YOU'RE REALLY DEAD NOW!! *(A gun is cocked. Marisol dives for cover. The Angel reacts. Sud-denly, the stage is blasted with white light. There's complete silence: the rattling, banging, screaming all stop. We hear crickets. Marisol, amazed by the instant calm, goes to the door, looks through the peephole. She cau-tiously opens the door. There's a small pile of salt on the floor. At first, Marisol just looks at it, too amazed to move. Then she bends down to touch the salt, letting it run through her fingers.)*

MARISOL. Salt? *(Frightened, not sure she knows what this means, Marisol quickly closes and locks the door. She gets into bed and turns out the light. Lights down everywhere except on the Angel.)*

Scene 4

Lights shift in Marisol's apartment as the Angel climbs down the ladder to Marisol's bed.

Marisol feels the tremendous heat given off by the Angel. The Angel backs away from Marisol so as not to burn her. The Angel goes to the window and looks out. Her voice is slightly amplified. She speaks directly to Marisol, who sleeps.

Throughout the scene, the light coming in through Marisol's window goes up slowly, until, by the end, it's the next morning.

ANGEL. A man is worshipping a fire hydrant on Taylor Avenue, Marisol. He's draping rosaries on it, genuflecting hard. An old woman's selling charmed chicken blood in see-through Ziplock bags for a buck. They're setting another homeless man on fire in Van Cortlandt Park. *(The Angel rattles the metal gate.)* Cut that shit out you fucking Nazis! *(The Angel goes to Marisol's door and checks the lock. She stomps cockroaches. She straightens up a little.)* I swear, best thing that could happen to this city is immediate evacuation followed by fire on a massive scale. Melt it all down. Consume the ruins. Then put the ashes of those evaporated dreams into a big urn and sit the urn on the desks of a few thousand oily politicians. Let them smell the disaster like we do. *(The Angel goes to Marisol's bed and looks at her. Marisol's heart beats faster and she starts to hyperventilate.)* So what do you believe in, Marisol? You believe in me? Or do you believe your senses? If so, what's that taste in your mouth? *(The Angel clicks her fingers.)*
MARISOL. *(In her sleep, tasting.)* Oh my God, *arroz con gandules!* Yum!
ANGEL. What's your favorite smell, Marisol? *(Click!)*
MARISOL. *(In her sleep, sniffing.)* The ocean! I smell the ocean!
ANGEL. Do you like sex, Marisol? *(Click! Marisol is seized by powerful sexual spasms that wrack her body and nearly throw her off the bed. When they end, Marisol stretches out luxuriously: exhausted but happy.)*

15

MARISOL. *(Laughing.)* I've got this wild energy running through my body! *(The Angel gets closer to her.)*

ANGEL. Here's your big chance, baby. What would you like to ask the Angel of the Lord?

MARISOL. *(In her sleep, energized.)* Are you real? Are you true? Are you gonna make the Bronx safe for me? Are you gonna make miracles and reduce my rent? Is it true angels' favorite food is Thousand Island dressing? Is it true your shit smells like mangos and when you're drunk you speak Portuguese?!

ANGEL. Honey, last time *I* was drunk ... *(Marisol gets a sudden, horrifying realization.)*

MARISOL. *Wait a minute — am I dead?* Did I die tonight? How did I miss that? Was it the man with the golf club? Did he beat me to death? Oh my God. I've been dead all night. And when I look around I see that Death is my ugly apartment in the Bronx. No this can't be Death! Death can't have this kind of furniture!

ANGEL. God, you're so cute, I could eat you up. No. You're still alive. *(Marisol is momentarily relieved — then she suddenly starts touching her stomach as she gets a wild, exhilarating idea.)*

MARISOL. *(In her sleep.) Am I pregnant with the Lord's baby?!* Is the new Messiah swimming in my electrified womb? Is the supersperm of God growing a mythic flower deep in the secret greenhouse inside me? Will my morning sickness taste like communion wine? This is amazing — *billions* of women on earth, and I get knocked up by God!

ANGEL. No baby, no baby, no baby, no baby — No. Baby. *(Beat. Marisol is a little disappointed.)*

MARISOL. *(In her sleep.)* No? Then what is it? Are you real or not? 'Cause if you're real and God is real and the Gospels are real, this would be the perfect time to tell me. 'Cause I once looked for angels, I did, in every shadow of my childhood — but I never found any. I thought I'd find you hiding inside the notes I sang to myself as a kid. The songs that put me to sleep and kept me from killing myself with fear. But I didn't see you then. *(The Angel doesn't answer. Her silence — her very presence — starts to unhinge Marisol.)* C'mon! Somebody up there has to tell me why I live the way I do! What's going *on* here, anyway? Why is there a war on children in this city? Why are apples extinct? Why are they planning to drop human insecticide on overpopulated areas of the Bronx? Why has the color blue disappeared from the sky? Why does common rainwater turn your skin bright red? Why do cows give salty milk? Why did the Plague kill half my friends? AND WHAT HAPPENED TO THE MOON? Where did the moon go? How come nobody's seen it in nearly *nine months...?* *(Marisol is trying desperately to keep from crying. The Angel gets into bed with Marisol. Contact with the Angel makes Marisol gasp. She opens her mouth to scream, but nothing comes out. Marisol collapses — her whole body goes limp. Marisol rests her head on the Angel's lap. Electricity surges gently through Marisol's body. She is feeling no pain, fear or loneliness. The Angel strokes her hair.)*

ANGEL.   I kick-started your heart, Marisol. I wired your nervous system. I pushed your fetal blood in the right direction and turned the foam in your infant lungs to oxygen. When you were six and your parents were fighting, I helped you pretend you were underwater: that you were a cold-blooded fish, in the bottom of the black ocean, far away and safe. When racists ran you out of school at ten, screaming ...

MARISOL.   *(In her sleep.)* ... "kill the spik ..."

ANGEL.   ... I turned the monsters into little columns of salt! At last count, one plane crash, one collapsed elevator, one massacre at the hands of a right-wing fanatic with an Uzi, and sixty-six-thousand-six-hundred-and-three separate sexual assaults never happened because of me.

MARISOL.   *(In her sleep.)* Wow. Now I don't have to be so paranoid...?* *(The Angel suddenly gets out of bed. Marisol curls up in a fetal position. The Angel is nervous now, full of hostile energy, anxious.)*

ANGEL.   Now the bad news. *(The Angel goes to the window. She's silent a moment as she contemplates the devastated Bronx landscape.)*

MARISOL.   *(In her sleep, worried.)* What? *(The Angel finds it very hard to tell Marisol what's on her mind.)*

ANGEL.   I can't expect you to understand the political ins and outs of what's going on. But you have eyes. You asked me questions about children and water and war and the moon: the same questions I've been asking myself for a thousand years. *(We hear distant explosions. Marisol's body responds with a jolt.)*

MARISOL.   *(In her sleep, quiet.)* What's that noise?

ANGEL.   The universal body is sick, Marisol. Constellations are wasting away, the nauseous stars are full of blisters and sores, the infected earth is running a temperature, and everywhere the universal mind is wracked with amnesia, boredom and neurotic obsessions.

MARISOL.   *(In her sleep, frightened.)* Why?

ANGEL.   Because God is old and dying and taking the rest of us with Him. And for too long, much too long, I've been looking the other way. Trying to stop the massive hemorrhage with my little hands. With my prayers. But it didn't work and I knew if I didn't do something soon, it would be too late.

MARISOL.   *(In her sleep, frightened.)* What did you do?

ANGEL.   I called a meeting. And I urged the Heavenly Hierarchies — the Seraphim, Cherubim, Thrones, Dominions, Principalities, Powers, Virtues, Archangels and Angels — to vote to stop the universal ruin ... by slaughtering our senile God. And they did. Listen well, Marisol: Angels are going to kill the King of Heaven and restore the vitality of the universe with His blood. And I'm going to lead them. *(Marisol takes this in silently — then suddenly erupts — her body shaking with fear and energy.)*

MARISOL.   *(In her sleep.)* Okay, I wanna wake up now!

ANGEL.   There's going to be war. A revolution of angels.

MARISOL.   *(In her sleep.)* GOD IS GREAT! GOD IS GOOD! THANK YOU FOR OUR NEIGHBORHOOD!

ANGEL.   Soon we're going to send out spies, draft able-bodied celestial beings, raise taxes ...

MARISOL.   *(In her sleep.)* THANK YOU FOR THE BIRDS THAT SING! THANK YOU GOD FOR EVERYTHING!

ANGEL.   Soon we're going to take off our wings of peace, Marisol, and put on our wings of war. Then we're going to spread blood and vigor across the sky and reawaken the dwindling stars!

MARISOL.   *(In her sleep, reciting fast.)* "And there was war in Heaven; Michael and his angels fought against the dragon; and the dragon fought — "

ANGEL.   It could be suicide. A massacre. He's better armed. Better organized. And, well, a little omniscient. But we *have* to

18

win. *(Beat.)* And when we do win ... when we crown the new God, and begin the new millennium ... the earth will be restored. The moon will return. The degradation of the animal kingdom will end. Men and women will be elevated to a higher order. All children will speak Latin. And Creation will finally be perfect. *(Distant thunder and lightning. The Angel quickly goes to the window to read the message in the lightning. She turns to Marisol, who is struggling to wake up.)* It also means I have to leave you. I can't stay. I can't protect you anymore. *(Beat.)*

MARISOL. *(In her sleep.)* What? You're *leaving* me?

ANGEL. I don't want to. I love you. I thought you had to know. But now I have to go and fight —

MARISOL. *(In her sleep.)* I'm going to be alone?

ANGEL. And that's what you have to do, Marisol. You have to fight. You can't *endure* anymore. You can't trust luck or prayer or mercy or other people. When I drop my wings, all hell's going to break loose and soon you're not going to recognize the world — so get yourself some *power*, Marisol, whatever you do.

MARISOL. *(In her sleep.)* What's going to happen to me without you...? *(The Angel goes to Marisol and tries to kiss her.)*

ANGEL. I don't know. *(Marisol lashes out, trying to hit the Angel. Marisol spits at the Angel. The Angel grabs Marisol's hands.)*

MARISOL. *I'm gonna be meat!* I'M GONNA BE FOOD!! *(By now the lights are nearly up full: it's the next morning. The Angel holds the struggling Marisol.)*

ANGEL. Unless you want to join us —

MARISOL. NOOOOO!! *(Marisol fights. Her alarm clock goes off. The Angel lets Marisol go and climbs up the ladder and disappears. Marisol wakes up violently — she looks around in a panic — instantly goes for the knife under her pillow. It takes her a few moments to realize she's home in her bed. She puts the knife away. Turns off the alarm clock. She thinks: "I must have been dreaming." She shakes her head, catches her breath and tries to calm down. She wipes the sweat from her face. Marisol gets out of bed. She goes to the window and looks down at the street — her eyes filled with new terror. She runs to her offstage bathroom.)*

Scene 5

Lights up on Marisol's office in Manhattan: two metal desks facing each other covered in books and papers. One desk has a small radio.

June enters the office. She's an Irish-American, 36: bright, edgy, hyper, dressed in cool East Village clothes. Her wild red hair and all-American freckles provide a vivid contrast to Marisol's Latin darkness. June tries to read the New York Post *but she can't concentrate. She keeps waiting for Marisol to appear. June turns on the radio.*

RADIO VOICE.   ... sources indicate the President's psychics believe they know where the moon has gone to. They claim to see the moon hovering over the orbit of Saturn, looking lost. Pentagon officials are considering plans to spend billions on a space tug to haul the moon back to earth. The tug would attach a long chain to the moon so it never strays from its beloved earth again. One insider has been quoted as saying the White House hopes to raise revenues for Operation Moon Rescue by taxing lunatics. Responding to allegations that cows are giving salty milk because grass is contaminated, government scientists are drafting plans to develop a new strain of cow that lives by eating Astroturf. *(June turns off the radio. Marisol enters the office in a change of clothes. June sees her and lets out a yell of joy. She goes to Marisol and embraces her.)*

JUNE.   Marisol! Thank God! I couldn't sleep all night because of you! *(Marisol, still shaken by the night's strange visions, is dazed, unhappy. She pulls away from June.)*

MARISOL.   *(Wary.)* What's the matter?

JUNE.   *(Grabbing her.)* You died! You died! It was all over the networks last night! You're on the front page of the *Post!* *(June shows Marisol the paper. On the cover is a closeup of a young woman's battered corpse. June reads.)* "*Twenty-six*-year-old *Marisol Perez* of

180th Street in the Bronx was bludgeoned to death on the IRT Number Two last night. The attack occurred 11:00 PM." *(Marisol tries to remain calm as she looks at the hideous picture.) I thought it was you.* And I tried to call you last night but do you have any idea how many Marisol Perezes there are in the Bronx phone book? Only seven pages. I couldn't sleep.

MARISOL. *(Barely calm.)* How did he kill her?

JUNE. Fucking barbarian beat her with a *golf club,* can you believe that? Like a caveman kills its *dinner,* fucking freak. I'm still upset. *(Marisol, numb, gives the paper back to June.)*

MARISOL. It wasn't me, June.

JUNE. It could have been you, living alone in that marginal neighborhood, all the chances you take. Like doesn't this scare you? Isn't it past time to leave the Bronx behind? *(Marisol looks at June fully for the first time, trying to focus her thoughts.)*

MARISOL. But it wasn't me. I didn't die last night. *(Marisol sits at her desk. June looks at the paper.)*

JUNE. *(Not listening.)* Goddamn vultures are having a field day with this, vast closeups of Marisol Perez's pummeled face on TV, I mean what's the *point?* There's a prevailing sickness out there, I'm telling you, the Dark Ages are here, Visigoths are climbing the city walls, and I've never felt more like raw food in my life. Am I upsetting you with this? *(Marisol rubs her throbbing head.)*

MARISOL. Yeah.

JUNE. Good. Put the fear of God in you. Don't let them catch you not ready, okay? You gotta be prepared to really *fight* now!

MARISOL. *(Looks at her, surprised.)* Why do you say that? Did somebody tell you to say that? *(June gives Marisol a long look.)*

JUNE. Something wrong with you today? You look like shit. You, Miss Puerto Rican Yuppy Princess of the Universe, you never look like shit. *(Marisol tries to smile, to shake off her fear.)*

MARISOL. It's nothing. Let's get to work. If I don't get this manuscript off my desk ... *(Marisol opens up a manuscript and tries to read it. June closes the manuscript.)*

JUNE. Something happen to you last night?

MARISOL. No — it's — nothing — it's — *my body* — it feels

like. Like it fits into my clothes all wrong today. Every person on the subway this morning gave me the shivers. They all looked so hungry. I keep hearing children crying. I keep smelling burnt flesh. And now there's a woman with my exact name killed on my exact street last night. *(Beat.)* And I had this dream. A winged woman. A black angel with beautiful wings. She came to my bed and said she loved me.

JUNE. *(Very interested.)* Oh?

MARISOL. She seemed so real. So absolute. Virtuous and powerful, incapable of lying, exalted, sublime, radiant, pure, perfect, fulgent.

JUNE. Fulgent? *(June takes Marisol by the shoulders and looks in her eyes.)* Whoa! Marisol! Yo! That didn't happen. You dreamed it. It's Roman Catholic bullshit.

MARISOL. ... now I feel sorry. I just feel so sorry for everything ... *(Marisol goes D. and looks up at the sky, expecting to see something, but not knowing what. She's fighting tears. June looks at her: Marisol's definitely not herself today. June goes to her, embraces her. Marisol holds June for dear life. June tries to cheer Marisol up.)*

JUNE. Lookit, I think your dream is like the moon's disappearance. It's all a lot of pre-millennium jitters. I've never seen so much nervousness. It's still up there but paranoia has clouded our view. That shit can happen you know. *(Marisol pulls away from June.)*

MARISOL. I don't think the moon's disappearance is psychological. It's like the universe is senile, June. Like we're at the part of history where everything breaks down. Do you smell smoke? *(The lights begin to subtly go down. June notices the darkness right away. She looks at her watch.)*

JUNE. Wait! It's nine-thirty! They're expecting the smoke from that massive fire in Ohio to reach New York by nine-thirty. *(June and Marisol look out the window. The lights go darker and darker.)* Jesus! Those are a million trees burning! *(June and Marisol calmly watch the spectacle.)* Christ, you can smell the polyester ... the burnt malls ... the defaulted loans ... the unemployment ... the flat vowels ... *(Lights begin to go up. Marisol and June stand at the window and watch the black smoke begin to drift toward Europe. Silence. They look at each other. The whole thing suddenly strikes them as absurd — they laugh.)* Fuck it, I'm going on break. You want something from downstairs? Coffee? I'm going for coffee.

MARISOL.   Coffee's extinct, June.

JUNE.   *(She hates tea.)* Tea — I meant *tea.* I'll get us both a cup of tea, try to carry on like normal. I swear, one more natural cataclysm like that and I'm going home. Are you okay? *(Marisol nods yes. June leaves the office. Marisol quickly starts reading from her manuscript.)*

MARISOL.   *(With growing surprise.)* "... Salt is in the food and mythology of cultures old and new. Ancient writers believed that angels in heaven turned into salt when they died. Popular mythology holds that during the Fall of Satan, angels who were killed in battle fell into the primordial ocean, which was then fresh water. Today, the oceans are salted by the decomposed bodies of fallen angels ..." *(The Man With Ice Cream enters the office. He wears a business suit and licks an ice cream cone. He smiles at Marisol, who looks at him, instantly sensing trouble.)*

ICE CREAM.   I was in the movie *Taxi Driver* with Robert De Niro and the son-of-a-gun never paid me.

MARISOL.   Uhm. Are you looking for someone?

ICE CREAM.   The Second A.D. said this is where I go to collect my pay for my work in *Taxi Driver.*

MARISOL.   This isn't a film company, sir. We publish science books. I think there's a film company on the tenth floor.

ICE CREAM.   No, this is the place. I'm sure this is the place.

MARISOL.   Well ... you know, sir ... maybe if I called security for you ...

ICE CREAM.   I worked real hard on that picture. It was my big break. And of course, working with a genius like De Niro is like Actor Heaven, but, c'mon, I still need the money!

MARISOL.   I'm a busy woman, sir, I have a department to run —

ICE CREAM.   I mean, I don't want to get temperamental, but *Taxi Driver* came out a long time ago and I still haven't been paid!

MARISOL.   Yeah, I'll call security for you —

ICE CREAM.   *(In despair.)* Christ, I have bills! I have rent! I have a toddler in a Catholic preschool! I have an agent screaming for his ten percent! *And how the fuck am I supposed to pay for this ice cream cone? Do you think ice cream is free? Do you think Carvel gives this shit out for nothing?*

MARISOL. *(Calling out.)* June?! Is somebody on this floor?!

ICE CREAM. Don't fuck with me, lady. I once played a Nazi skinhead in a TV movie-of-the-week. I once set a man on fire in Van Cortlandt Park for CBS! *And I really liked that role! (The Man throws the ice cream into Marisol's face. June runs on.)*

JUNE. LEAVE HER ALONE YOU SCUMBAG! *(June hits the Man as hard as she can. She pummels him. He howls like a dog and runs out of the office. June runs after him. Off.)* SOMEBODY HELP ME GET HIM! (As Marisol wipes the ice cream from her face, we hear footsteps going into the distance. Then footsteps returning. June runs back in, panting.)* He's gone. *(June picks up the phone.)* Security? *YOU FUCKING BOZOS!* WHY DON'T YOU DO YOUR JOB AND STOP LETTING MANIACS INTO THE BUILDING?! *(June slams down the phone. She goes to Marisol, who is still wiping ice cream from her clothes. She's trembling.)*

MARISOL. Vanilla almond. I'll never be able to eat vanilla almond again.

JUNE. Okay, that's IT, you and I are taking the rest of the day off, going to my house where it's *safe, fuck* everybody, I've had it with this deathtrap ... *(June starts to hustle Marisol out of the office. Marisol looks up — she's frozen by a vision. Lights up, far above Marisol. The Angel is there, cleaning an Uzi submachine gun, humming quietly. Marisol isn't sure she's really seeing what she's seeing. June looks up, sees nothing, and pulls Marisol offstage. Lights down on the Angel, who disappears in the dark.)*

Scene 6

Lights up on June's apartment: a marbleized Formica table and matching red chairs.

It's later that day. June and Marisol enter. June automatically stomps cockroaches as she enters.

JUNE.   ... so we agitated for them to install metal detectors in all the buildings on this block. That'll definitely cut down on the random homicides.

MARISOL.   That's civilized.

JUNE.   *(Brightly.)* That's Brooklyn.

MARISOL.   What's that huge ugly windowless building with the smokestacks and armed guards across the street?

JUNE.   Me? I think it's where they bring overthrown brutal right-wing dictators from Latin America to live, 'cause a friend's a friend, right?

MARISOL.   I really appreciate this, June.

JUNE.   Good, 'cause now I have to issue you a warning about my fucked-up brother who lives with me.

MARISOL.   You do?

JUNE.   Uhm. Lenny's a little weird about women. His imagination? It takes off on him on the slightest provocation and, uh, he doesn't know, you know, a reasonable way to channel his turbulent sexual death fantasies ...

MARISOL.   This is a long warning, June.

JUNE.   He knows about you. Shit I've told him for two years. And so he's developed this *thing* for you, like he draws *pictures* of you, in crayon, covering every inch of his bedroom. He's thirty-four, you know, but he has the mental capacity of a child. *(Lenny enters. Lenny has uncontrollable hair that makes him look a little crazy. He can stand very, very still for a very long time. He goes immediately to the window without looking at June or Marisol.)*

LENNY.   *(Indicating window.)* Wrong. It's a federally funded torture center where they violate people who have gone over their credit card limit.

JUNE.   *(Wary.)* Marisol, this is Lenny, the heat-seeking device. Lenny, this is Marisol Perez and you're *wrong*.

LENNY.   *(At window.)* I've seen them bring the vans, June. So shut up. People tied up. Guards with truncheons. Big fat New York City police with dogs. It happens late at night. But you can hear the screams. They cremate the bodies. That's why Brooklyn smells so funny.

MARISOL.   *(Nervous.)* I owe a lot of money to the MasterCard people. *(Lenny suddenly turns to Marisol. He is utterly focused on her.)*

JUNE. *(To Marisol.)* What he says is not proven.

LENNY. *Everybody* knows, June. It's a political *issue.* If you weren't so right-wing —

JUNE. I am not right-wing, you punk, don't EVER call me that! I happen to be the last true practicing communist in New York! *(Lenny keeps staring at Marisol.)*

LENNY. You were on the news. You died on the news. But that was a different one.

MARISOL. She and I have the same name. Had.

LENNY. *(Approaching Marisol.)* I'm so glad you didn't die before I got a chance to meet you. *(Lenny suddenly takes Marisol's hand and kisses it June tries to step in between them.)*

JUNE. That's enough, Lenny — I didn't bring her here to feed on ...

LENNY. *(Holding Marisol's hand.)* I went to your neighborhood this morning. To see the kind of street that would kill a Marisol Perez. I walked through Van Cortlandt Park. I played in the winter sunlight, watched perverts fondling snowmen, and at high noon, the dizziest time of the day, I saw a poor homeless guy being set on fire by Nazi skinheads —

JUNE. That's *it,* Lenny. *(June pulls Lenny aside. He knows he's in for a lecture.)*

LENNY. What?

JUNE. We had a hard day. We came here to relax. So take a deep breath —

LENNY. She talked to me first —

JUNE. Listen to me before you say anything more. Are you listening — ?

LENNY. *Yes. Okay.*

JUNE. Let's cool our hormones, okay? Before the psychodrama starts in earnest — ?

LENNY. Yes. All right.

JUNE. Are we really — ? *(Lenny pulls away from June.)*

LENNY. *(To Marisol.)* Hey, honey, you wanna see my sculpture? *(Lenny runs to his offstage bedroom before Marisol can reply. June grabs her coat angrily.)*

JUNE. You wanna get outta here? He's raving.

LENNY. *(Off.)* I'm an accomplished sculptor, Marisol. Before that I was a Life and Growth Empowerment Practitioner. Before that I worked for the Brooklyn Spiritual Emergence Network. *(Lenny quickly reenters with his sculpture, a ball of nails welded together in a formless shape: it's an ugly little work of art and everyone knows it.)* This one's called "Marisol Perez." The nails symbolize all the things I know about you. Spaces between the nails are all the things I don't know about you. As you see, you're a great mystery ... *(Marisol looks at the sculpture, trying hard to see some beauty in it.)* No one else is working like this. It's totally new. But it's only a small step in my career. I'm going to need a lot more money if I'm going to evolve past this point. *(Lenny looks hard at June. June buttons up her coat, hoping to avoid a confrontation.)*
JUNE. *(Tight.)* I don't think Marisol wants to hear us talk about money.
LENNY. Well, I'm not gonna get a job, June, so you can fuck that noise.
JUNE. *(To Marisol.)* Who said "job"? When did I say "job" — ?
LENNY. *(To Marisol.)* I promised myself to never work for anyone again. She heard me say that —
JUNE. Gee Lenny, fuck you, we're going — *(June starts to go. Lenny blocks her path to the door.)*
LENNY. *(To June.)* Why do you hate my sculpture? Why do you hate everything I do?!
JUNE. *(Trying to control herself.)* Man, man ... Lenny ... you don't want to learn *anything* from me, do you? You want to be a pathetic invertebrate your whole life long. Fine. Just don't waste my precious time!
LENNY. Who gives a fuck about your time, I HAVE PROJECTS!
JUNE. Yeah? What ever happened to the CIA, Lenny? Didn't they want you for something *really special* in Nicaragua? What about the electric guitars you were gonna design for the Stones? What about *Smegma, the Literary Magazine of Brooklyn?* Huh? *(Lenny runs back into his offstage room.)* I swear, the cadavers of your dead projects are all over this goddamn apartment like Greenwood Cemetery. I can't eat a bowl of cereal in the

27

morning without the ghosts of your old ideas begging me for a glass of milk! *(Lenny reenters with stacks of homemade magazines and several unusual homemade guitars. He throws this trash at June's feet.)*

LENNY. *You wish Mom had drowned me!* I know that's what you wish! Well, you don't have to feel sorry for me anymore!

JUNE. Sure I do. You're pathetic. The only thing separating you from a concrete bed on Avenue D is *me*.

LENNY. *(To Marisol.)* She thinks I'm a loser, Marisol! Can you believe that? Sometimes I want to kill her!

JUNE. Oh get out of my face, Lenny. You're never gonna kill me. You're never gonna get it together to kill *anybody* — *(Lenny exits into his offstage room again. June turns to Marisol angrily.)* Can I list for you just a few of the things I don't have because I have him? Lasting friendships. A retirement account. A house. A career. A nightlife. Winter clothing. Interest on checking. Regular real sex. *(Lenny returns with a long kitchen knife and tries to cut June's throat. June and Marisol scream.)*

LENNY. *I was supposed to be somebody!* That's what I learned right after I died!

JUNE. YOU NEVER DIED — ! *(June scrambles from Lenny and goes for the door. There's chaos as Marisol starts throwing things at Lenny and Lenny continues to chase June. Lenny pulls June from the door and throws her back in the room.)*

LENNY. The doctors all said I died! There's medical evidence! It's on the charts! My heart stopped for seven minutes and my soul was outta Lenox Hill at the speed of light! *(Lenny is almost out of control as he stalks June, slashing the air.)*

JUNE. Your whole *life*, everything I do is to *bolster* you, build you up —

LENNY. After my death ... my soul was cruising up and up ... and it was intercepted by angels and sucked back into my body, *and I lived!*

MARISOL. Give me that knife!

LENNY. ... I was resurrected, I returned to the living to warn the world that big changes are coming ... and we have to be ready ... *(Fighting tears.)* ... I've been warning people for years, but no one listens to me ... *(Lenny starts to cry. Marisol and June jump him, grabbing the knife away. Lenny throws himself on the ground like a toddler in a rage and cries. June and Marisol look at him. It takes June a moment to catch her breath and gather her thoughts.)*

JUNE.   I can't do this shit no more. I can't mother you. Carry you around protected in my Epic Uterus anymore. This is final. Biology says you're a grown man. I don't love the law of the jungle, Lenny, but you're adult, you're leaving the nest and living in the real world from now on, eat or be eaten, I'm sorry, that's the way my emotions are built right now 'cause you *architectured* it that way! *(Beat.)* I'm calling our mother, tell her not to take you in either. This is not a transition, Leonard. This is a break. A severing. So get up. Collect your mutant trash. Give me your fucking keys. Leave right now. And don't look back at me or I'll turn you to salt right where you stand with my eyes, so help me God. *(Lenny stands, gathers his trash, and exits to his room. Marisol goes to comfort June, but she's interrupted by Lenny reentering, wearing a coat, carrying a bag of golf clubs. June gives Lenny all the money she has on her. Marisol is unable to look at Lenny. He turns angrily to June.)*

LENNY.   I almost had Marisol married to me, June. We practically had babies! Now I'm alone. Whatever happens to me out there, it's totally, specifically, on you. *(Lenny leaves the apartment. June sits at the table. Marisol looks at June.)*

MARISOL.   So where do you want to have dinner? *(No answer. Marisol sits with June, takes her hand. Tears on June's face.)*

JUNE.   You think I'm a shit for throwing him out...?

MARISOL.   Maybe people will throw him some change. Maybe this will force him to get a job.

JUNE.   ... is he gonna dissolve in the fucking street air...? *(June runs to the door. She calls out.)* Lenny! I'm SORRY! Come back, I'm sorry!! *(No answer. June sits.)* Shit. *(June looks at Marisol, wiping her tears, getting an idea.)* You wanna live with me? 'Cause if you wanna live with me, in Lenny's empty bedroom, I'll rent it to you, it's available right away. *(Marisol smiles, surprised.)*

MARISOL.   Wait — where did that come from?

JUNE.   Hey c'mon girlfriend, they're killing Marisol Perezes left and right today, we gotta stick together!

MARISOL.   *(Wanting to.)* Wow. I don't know what to say ...

JUNE. You think the Bronx needs you? It doesn't. It needs blood. It needs to feed. You *wanna* be the blood supply for its filthy habits?

MARISOL. But the Bronx is where I'm from.

JUNE. So friggin' what? Come here. We'll survive the millennium as a team. I'll shop. You can clean the chemicals off the food. I know where to buy gas masks. You know the vocabulary on the street. We'll walk each other through land mines and sharpen each other's wits. *(Marisol smiles and looks at June.)*

MARISOL. You're not saying that just because you're scared to be alone, right? You really want me here, right?

JUNE. Of course I do, hey.

MARISOL. Then let's do it, girlfriend. *(Delighted, June embraces Marisol.)*

JUNE. Oh great! *(June and Marisol hold each other. June is about ready to cry. Marisol gently rocks her a little bit, then looks at June.)*

MARISOL. I'm gonna go home and pack right now. We have to be fast. This town knows when you're alone. That's when it sends out the ghouls and the death squads. *(June nods understandingly, kisses Marisol and gives her Lenny's keys.)*

JUNE. What a day I'm having, huh? *(Marisol takes the keys, leaves, goes back to her own apartment and immediately starts packing.)*

Scene 7

Later that night. Marisol is in the Bronx packing. Her singing is heard underneath the others' dialogue.

MARISOL. *(Softly.) Madre que linda noche, cuantas estrellas. Abreme la ventana, que quiero verlas ... (June sits at the table in her apartment, facing D. She talks to herself.)*

JUNE. Maybe someone'll throw Lenny some change, right? *(Lenny appears U., on the street, warming his hands at a burning trash can. His clothes are filthy and his eyes are glazed. The golf club is at his side. He looks at Marisol.)*

LENNY.   I've been on the street, Marisol. I know what it's like.

JUNE.   Yeah, maybe people will throw him some change.

MARISOL.   *(Smiling, remembering.)* "The flat vowels ..."

LENNY.   It's incredible there. Logic was executed by firing squad. People tell passionate horror stories and other people stuff their faces and go on. The street breeds new species. And new silence. No spoken language works there. There are no verbs to describe the cold air as it sucks on your hands. And if there *were* words to describe it, Marisol, you wouldn't believe it anyway, because, in fact, it's literally unbelievable, it's another reality, and it's actually happening *right now*. And *that* fact — the fact that it's happening right *now* — compounds the unbelievable nature of the street, Marisol, adds to its lunacy, its permanent deniability. *(Beat.)* But I know it's real. I've been bitten by it. I have its rabies.

JUNE.   I know someone will throw him some change. *(Lenny raises the golf club over June's head. June is frozen. Blackout everywhere but Marisol's apartment. June and Lenny exit in the dark.)*

Scene 8

There's loud knocking at Marisol's door. Marisol stops packing and looks at the door. The knocking continues — loud, violent — louder.

MARISOL.   Who is it? *(Before Marisol can move, her door is kicked open. Lenny comes in wielding a bloody golf club and holding an armful of exotic wildflowers.)*

LENNY.   So how can you live in this neighborhood? Huh? You got a death wish, you stupid woman?

MARISOL.   What are you doing here? *(Marisol goes to her bed and scrambles for the knife underneath her pillow.)*

LENNY. Don't you love yourself? Is that why you stay in this ghetto? Jesus, I almost got killed getting here! *(Marisol points the knife at Lenny.)*

MARISOL. Get out or I'll rip out both your fucking eyes, Lenny!

LENNY. God, I missed you. *(Lenny closes the door and locks all the locks.)*

MARISOL. This is not going to happen to me in my own house! I still have God's protection! *(Lenny holds out the flowers.)*

LENNY. Here. I hadda break into the Bronx Botanical Garden for them, but they match your eyes ... *(Lenny hands Marisol the flowers.)*

MARISOL. Okay — thank you — okay — why don't we — turn around — and go — down to Brooklyn — okay? — let's go talk to June —

LENNY. We can't. Impossible. June *isn't*. Is *not*. I don't know who she is anymore! She's out walking the streets of Brooklyn! Babbling like an idiot! Looking for her lost mind!

MARISOL. What do you mean? Where is she?

LENNY. She had an accident. Her head had an accident. With the golf club. It was weird.

MARISOL. *(Looking at the bloody club.)* What did you do to her?

LENNY. She disappeared! I don't know!

MARISOL. *(Panicking.)* Please tell me June's okay, Lenny. Tell me she's not in some body bag somewhere —

LENNY. Oh man, you saw what it's like! June *controlled* me. She had me *neutered*. I squatted and stooped and served like a goddamn house eunuch!

MARISOL. Did you hurt her — ? *(Lenny starts to cry. He sobs like a baby, his body wracked with grief and self-pity.)*

LENNY. There are whole histories of me you can't guess. Did you know I was a medical experiment? To fix my asthma when I was five, my mother volunteered me for a free experimental drug on an army base in Nevada. *I was a shrieking experiment in army medicine for six years!* Isn't that funny? *(He laughs, trying to fight his tears.)* And that drug's made me so friggin' loopy, I can't hold down a job, make friends, get a degree, *nothing* — and June? — June's had *everything*. She loved you. That's why she never brought you home to meet me *even after I begged her for two years. (Marisol is silent — and that silence nearly makes him explode.)* DON'T BE THIS WAY. We don't have to be enemies. We can talk to each other the right way —

MARISOL. We have no right way, Lenny. *(Lenny jumps up and down, very happy.)*

LENNY. We do! We do! 'Cause we have *God*, Marisol. We have God in common. Maybe it's God's will I'm with you now. On this frontier. Out in this lawless city, I'm what he designed for you.

MARISOL. I don't know what you're talking about ...

LENNY. It's why God brought me here tonight — to offer you a way to survive. I know you don't love me. But you can't turn your back on God's gift.

MARISOL. *(Exhausted.)* Jesus Christ, just tell me what you want ... *(Lenny moves closer.)*

LENNY. I want to offer you a deal. *(Beat.)* You controlled your life until now. But your life's in shambles! Ruins! So I'm gonna let you give *me* control over your life. That means I'll do everything for you. I'll take responsibility. I'll get a job and make money. I'll name our children. Okay? And what you get in return is my protection. *(Beat. Lenny gives Marisol the golf club.)* I can protect you like June did. I can keep out the criminals and carry the knife for you. I can be your guardian angel, Marisol.

MARISOL. You're asking —

LENNY. A small price. Your faith. Your pretty Puerto Rican smile. No. I don't even want to sleep with you anymore. I don't want your affection. Or your *considerable* sexual mystery. I just want you to look up to me. Make me big. Make me central. Praise me, feed me, and believe everything I tell you. *(Lenny steps closer to Marisol.)* You once tried to give these things to June. And June would have said yes because she loved you. Well, I'm June. June and I are here, together, under this hungry skin. You can love us both, Marisol. *(Marisol looks at Lenny a long moment, studying him, thinking of a way out. She makes a decision. She tosses her knife on the bed and drops the golf club. She takes a step toward Lenny. They stare at each other. Marisol lets herself be embraced. Lenny, amazed, revels in the feel of her body against his.)*

MARISOL. Okay. I'll believe what you say. I'll live inside you.

(Lenny is oblivious to everything but Marisol's warm hands. She kisses him. It's the most electrifying feeling Lenny's ever known. He closes his eyes.) But. Before we set up house — live happily ever after — we're going to go outside — you and me — and we're going to find out what happened to your sister ...

LENNY. *(Oblivious.)* She's lost. She can't be found.

MARISOL. *(Kissing him.)* ... that's my condition ... *(Lenny starts to push Marisol to the bed. She starts to resist.)*

LENNY. It's too dangerous for a girl out there.

MARISOL. ... but if you don't help me find her, Lenny ... there's no deal ... *(He pushes her. She resists. Lenny looks at her, hurt, a little confused.)*

LENNY. But I don't want to share you. *(Beat.)*

MARISOL. Too bad. That's the deal. *(Beat.)*

LENNY. *(Hurt, realizing.)* You don't love me. You're just fucking with me. That's not okay! WELL, I'M GLAD I HIT HER! *(Lenny grabs Marisol. Marisol tries to escape. They struggle. He holds her tightly, trying to kiss her. He throws her to the floor. He rips at her clothes, trying to tear them off. Marisol struggles with all her strength — until she finally pulls free, and goes for the golf club. He tries to grab it from her and she swings at him.)* You're lying to me! Why are you always lying to me?!

MARISOL. Because you're the enemy, Lenny. I will always be your enemy, because you will always find a way to be out there, hiding in stairwells, behind doors, under the blankets in my bed, in the cracks of every bad dream I've had since I've known there were savage differences between girls and boys! And I know you'll always be hunting for me. And I'll never be able to relax, or stop to look at the sky, or smile at something beautiful on the street —

LENNY. But I'm just a guy trying to be happy too —

MARISOL. I want you to tell me, RIGHT NOW, where June is — *right now!* *(Marisol swings at Lenny. He panics and falls to his knees in front of her. Marisol pounds the floor with the golf club.)*

LENNY. She's on the street.

MARISOL. Where?

LENNY. Brooklyn.

MARISOL. Where?

LENNY. I don't know!

MARISOL. What happened?

LENNY. I hit her on the head. She doesn't know who she is. She went out there to look for you. *(Marisol stands over him, poised to strike him. He's shaking with fear.)* Look at me. I'm a mess on the floor. Just asking you to look at me. To give me compassion and let me live like a human being for once. Marisol, we could have a baby ... and love it so much ...

(Marisol only shakes her head in disgust and turns to the door. Lenny springs to his feet and lunges at her. She turns and swings the club and hits Lenny. He falls to the ground. Marisol looks at Lenny's fallen body. Has she killed him? She panics and runs out of the apartment with the golf club. Blackout everywhere except on the street area.)

Scene 9

Marisol runs to the street area.

It starts to snow there. Lenny's blood is on Marisol's clothes. She's extremely cold. She shivers. She kneels on the ground, alone, not knowing what to do or where to go.

Lights up over Marisol's head, against the brick wall. The Angel appears. The Angel wears regulation military fatigues, complete with face camouflage and medals. She looks like a soldier about to go into battle. The Uzi is strapped to her back.

Marisol sees her and gasps.

There's blood coming down the Angel's back: the Angel has taken off her silver wings — her wings of peace. She holds the bloody wings out to the audience, like an offering. Then she drops the wings. They float down to the street.

Marisol picks them up.

MARISOL.   War? *(The wings dissolve in Marisol's hands. Blackout everywhere.)*

END OF ACT ONE

ACT TWO

Darkness. All the interiors are gone. The entire set now consists of the brick wall and a huge surreal street that covers the entire stage.

The Angel is gone. The gold crown still there.

Street lighting comes up: but there's something very different about this light. On this street, reality has been altered — and this new reality is reflected in the lighting.

We see a metal trash bin, overflowing with trash and a fire hydrant covered in rosaries. There are several large mounds of rags on stage; underneath each mound is a sleeping Homeless Person.

Marisol is onstage exactly where she was at the end of Act One. She's holding out her hands as if holding the Angel's wings: but they're gone now; she holds air.

She looks around and notices that the street she's now on is nothing like the street she remembers. She registers this weird difference and picks up the golf club, ready to defend herself.

She looks up to see the Angel, but she's gone.

She thinks she hears a sound behind her; she swings the club. There's nothing there. She tries to orient herself but she can't tell north from south.

And even though it's the dead of winter, it's also much warmer than it was before. Startled, Marisol fans herself.

Bright sparkling lights streak across the sky like tracers or comets. The lights are followed by distant rumblings. Is that a thunderclap? Or an explosion? Marisol hits the ground. Then the lights stop. Silence.

The Woman With Furs enters. The Woman is prosperous: long fur coat and high heels — but there are subtle bruises and cuts on her face, and it looks like there's dried blood on her coat. She stands to the side, very, very still. She holds an open newspaper, but she stares past it, no emotion on her shell-shocked face.

Marisol looks at the Woman With Furs, hesitates, then goes to her.

MARISOL. Excuse me. Miss? *(No answer from the Woman With Furs, who doesn't look at her.)* Where the hell are we? *(The Woman With Furs ignores her. Marisol gets closer.)* I'm — supposed to be on 180th Street. In the Bronx. There's supposed to be a bodega right *here*. A public school *there*. They sold crack on that corner. It was cold this morning! *(The Woman With Furs speaks out to the air, as if in a trance.)*
WOMAN WITH FURS. God help you, you get in my face. *(Marisol begins to examine the altered space with growing fear.)*
MARISOL. No buildings. No streets. No cars. No noise. No cops. There are no subway tokens in my pocket!
WOMAN WITH FURS. I have no money.
MARISOL. *(Realizing.)* It's what she said would happen, isn't it? She said she'd drop her wings of peace ... and I wouldn't recognize the world ...
WOMAN IN FURS. Don't you know where you are either?
MARISOL. *(Trying to think it through.)* ... I have to ... I have to ... reclaim what I know: I need June. Where's June? Brooklyn. South. I gotta go south, find my friend, and restore her broken mind. *(Marisol tries to run away, hoping to find the subway to Brooklyn, but it's impossible to find anything familiar in this radically altered landscape.)*

WOMAN WITH FURS. I had tickets to *Les Misérables*. But I took a wrong turn. Followed bad advice. Ended up on this weird street. *(Marisol sees something in the distance that makes her freeze in her tracks.)*

MARISOL. *(To herself.)* The Empire State Building? ... *what's it doing over there?* It's supposed to be south. But that's ... north ... I'm sure it is ... isn't it? *(In her panic, Marisol runs to the Woman With Furs and tries to grab her arm.)* You have to help me! *(The Woman With Furs instantly recoils from Marisol's touch. She starts to wander away.)*

WOMAN WITH FURS. I have to go. But I can't find a cab. I can't seem to find any transportation.

MARISOL. You're not listening! There's no transportation; forget that; the city's *gone.* You have to help me. We have to go south together and protect each other. *(Marisol grabs the Woman With Furs' arm roughly, trying to pull her offstage. The Woman With Furs seems to snap out of her trance and pull back. The Woman With Furs is suddenly shaking, tearful, like a caged animal.)*

WOMAN WITH FURS. Oh God, I thought you were a nice person — !

MARISOL. *(Grabbing the Woman.)* I *am* a nice person, but I've had some bad luck —

WOMAN WITH FURS. *(Struggling.)* Oh God, you're hurting me —

MARISOL. *(Letting go.)* No, no, no, I'm okay; I don't belong out here; I have a job in publishing; I'm middle-class —

WOMAN WITH FURS. *(Freaking out, pointing at golf club.)* Oh please don't kill me like that barbarian killed Marisol Perez! *(Marisol lets the Woman With Furs go. The Woman With Furs is almost crying.)*

MARISOL. I'm not what you think.

WOMAN WITH FURS. ... Oh God, why did I have to buy that fucking hat?! God ... God ... why?

MARISOL. Please. June's not used to the street, she's an indoor animal, like a cat ...

WOMAN WITH FURS. I bought a fucking hat on credit and everything disintegrated!

MARISOL.   South. Protection. *(The Woman With Furs takes off her fur coat. Underneath, she wears ripped pajamas. We can see the bruises and cuts on her arms clearly.)*

WOMAN WITH FURS.   There is no protection. I just got out of hell. Last month, I was two hundred dollars over my credit card limit because I bought a hat on sale. And you know they're cracking down on that kind of thing. I used to do it all the time. It didn't matter. But now it matters. Midnight. The police came. Grabbed me out of bed, waving my credit statement in my face, my children screaming, they punched my husband in the stomach. I told them I was a lawyer! With a house in Cos Cob! And personal references a mile long! But they hauled me to this ... huge windowless brick building in Brooklyn ... where they tortured me ... they ... *(The Woman With Furs cries. Marisol goes to her and covers her up with the fur coat. Marisol holds her.)*

MARISOL.   That can't happen.

WOMAN WITH FURS.   A lot of things can't happen that are happening. Everyone I know's had terrible luck this year. Losing condos. Careers cut in half. Ending up on the street. I thought I'd be immune. I thought I'd be safe.

MARISOL.   This is going to sound crazy. But I think I know why this is happening. *(The Woman With Furs looks at Marisol, suddenly very afraid.)*

WOMAN WITH FURS.   No. No. *(The Woman With Furs tries to get away from Marisol. Marisol stops her.)*

MARISOL.   It's angels, isn't it? It's the war.

WOMAN WITH FURS.   *(Panicking.)* God is great! God is good! It didn't happen! It didn't happen! I dreamed it! I lied!

MARISOL.   It did! It happened to me!

WOMAN WITH FURS.   I'm not going to talk about this! You're going to think I'm crazy too! You're going to tell the Citibank MasterCard people where I am so they can pick me up and torture me some more!

MARISOL.   I wouldn't! *(The Woman With Furs grabs the golf club out of Marisol's hand.)*

WOMAN WITH FURS.   I know what I'm going to do now. I'm going to turn *you* in. I'm going to tell the Citibank police you stole my plastic! They'll like me for that. They'll like me a lot. They'll restore my banking privileges! *(The Woman With Furs starts swinging wildly at Marisol. Marisol dodges the Woman With Furs.)*

MARISOL. I am not an animal! I am not a barbarian! I don't fight at this level!

WOMAN WITH FURS. *(Swinging.)* Welcome to the new world order, babe! *(The Man With Scar Tissue enters in a wheelchair. He's a homeless man in shredded, burnt rags. He wears a hood which covers his head and obscures his face. He wears sunglasses and gloves. His wheelchair is full of plastic garbage bags, clothes, books, newspapers, bottles, junk.)*

SCAR TISSUE. It's getting so bad, a guy can't sleep under the stars anymore. *(The Woman With Furs sees the Man With Scar Tissue and stops swinging.)*

WOMAN WITH FURS. *(Indicating Marisol.)* This brown piece of shit is mine! *I'm* going to turn her in! Not you!

SCAR TISSUE. I was sleeping under the constellations one night and my whole life changed, took *seconds:* I had a life — then bingo — I *didn't* have a life ... *(Scar Tissue moves toward the Woman With Furs.)* ... maybe you got it, huh? You got the thing I need ...

WOMAN WITH FURS. Homelessness is against the law in this city. I'm going to have you two arrested! They'll like that. I'll get big points for that! I'll be revitalized!

(The Woman With Furs runs off with the golf club. Scar Tissue looks at Marisol. He waves hello. She looks at him — wary, but grateful — and tries to smile. She's instantly aware of his horrendous smell.)

MARISOL. She, she was trying to kill me ... thank you ...

SCAR TISSUE. Used to be able to sleep under the moon *unmolested.* Moon was a shield. Catching all the bad karma before it fell to earth. All those crater holes in the moon? Those ain't rocks! That's bad karma crashing to the moon's surface!

MARISOL. *(Really shaken.)* She thinks I belong out here, but I don't. I'm well-educated ... anyone can see that ...

SCAR TISSUE. Now the moon's gone. The shield's been lifted. Shit falls on you randomly. Sleep outside, you're fucked. That's

41

why I got this! Gonna *yank* the moon back! *(From inside his wheel-chair, Scar Tissue pulls out a magnet. He aims his magnet to the sky and waits for the moon to appear.)*

MARISOL.   She's crazy, that's all! I have to go before she comes back. *(Marisol starts going back and forth, looking for south.)*

SCAR TISSUE.   Good thing I'm not planning to get married. What would a honeymoon be like now? Some stupid cardboard cut-out dangling out your hotel window? What kind of inspiration is that? How's a guy supposed to get it up for *that? (Scar Tissue fondles himself, hoping to manufacture a hard-on, but nothing happens and he gives up.)*

MARISOL.   *(Noticing what he's doing.)* I have to get to Brooklyn. I'm looking for my friend. She has red hair.

SCAR TISSUE.   And did you know the moon carries the souls of dead people up to Heaven? Uh-huh. The new moon is dark and empty and gets filled with new glowing souls — until it's a bright full moon — then it carries its silent burden to God ...

MARISOL.   Do you know which way is south?! *(Marisol continues to walk around and around the stage, looking hopelessly for any land-mark that will tell her which way is south. Scar Tissue watches her, holding his magnet up.)*

SCAR TISSUE.   Give it up, princess. Time is crippled. Geography's deformed. You're permanently lost out here!

MARISOL.   Bullshit. Even if God is senile, He still cares, He doesn't play dice you know. I read that.

SCAR TISSUE.   Shit, what century do *you* live in? *(Marisol keeps running around the stage.)*

MARISOL.   June and I had plans. Gonna live together. Survive together. I gotta get her fixed! I gotta get Lenny buried! *(Scar Tissue laughs and suddenly drops his magnet and jumps out of his wheelchair. He runs to Marisol, stopping her in her tracks. He looks at the shocked Marisol fully for the first time. He smiles, very pleased.)*

SCAR TISSUE.   You look pretty nice. You're kinda cute, in fact. What do you think this all means, us two, a man and woman, bumping into each other like this?

MARISOL.   *(Wary.)* I don't know. But thank you for helping me. Maybe my luck hasn't run out.

SCAR TISSUE. *(Laughs.)* Oh, don't trust luck! Fastest way to die around here. Trust gunpowder. Trust plutonium. Don't trust divine intervention or you're fucked. My name is Elvis Presley, beautiful, what's yours?

MARISOL. *(Wary.)* ... Marisol Perez. *(Scar Tissue nearly jumps out of his rags.)*

SCAR TISSUE. *What?!!* No! Your name can't be that! Can't be Marisol Perez!

MARISOL. It is. It has to be.

SCAR TISSUE. You're confused! Or are the goddamn graves coughing up the dead?!

MARISOL. I'm not dead! That was her! I'm — me!

SCAR TISSUE. You can't prove it!

MARISOL. I was born in the Bronx. But — but — I can't remember the street!

SCAR TISSUE. A-ha! Dead!

MARISOL. *(A recitation, an effort.)* Lived on East Tremont — then Taylor Avenue — Grand Concourse — Mami died — Fordham — English major — Phi Beta Kappa — I went into science publishing — I'm a head copywriter — I make good money — I work with words — I'm clean ... *(As Marisol holds her head and closes her eyes, Scar Tissue starts going through his bag, pulling out old magazines and newspapers.)* ... I lived in the Bronx ... I commuted light-years to this other planet called — Manhattan! I learned new vocabularies ... wore weird native dress ... mastered arcane rituals ... and amputated neat sections of my psyche, my cultural heritage ... yeah, clean easy amputations ... with no pain expressed at all — none! — but so much pain kept inside I almost choked on it ... so far deep inside my Manhattan bosses and Manhattan friends and my broken Bronx consciousness never even suspected ... *(Scar Tissue reads from the New York Post.)*

SCAR TISSUE. "Memorial services for Marisol Perez were held this morning in Saint Patrick's Cathedral. The estimated fifty thousand mourners included the Mayor of New York, the Bronx Borough President, the Guardian Angels and the cast of the popular daytime soap opera *As the World Turns* ..."

MARISOL. She wasn't me! I'm me! And I'm outta here! *(Marisol starts to run off — but is stopped as, far U., in the dark, a Nazi Skinhead, played by June, walks by, holding a can of gasoline, goose-stepping ominously toward a sleeping Homeless Person. Marisol runs back and hides behind Scar Tissue's wheelchair. The Skinhead doesn't see them. Scar Tissue sees the Skinhead and suddenly hides behind Marisol, shaking. He starts to whine and cry and moan. The Homeless Person runs off. The Skinhead exits, chasing the Homeless Person. When the Skinhead is gone, Scar Tissue turns angrily to Marisol.)*

SCAR TISSUE. Who are you for real and why do you attract so much trouble?! I hope you don't let those Nazis come near me!

MARISOL. I don't mean to — *(He grabs Marisol.)*

SCAR TISSUE. What are you!? Are you protection? Are you benign? Or are you some kind of angel of death?

MARISOL. I'm a good person.

SCAR TISSUE. Then why don't you do something about those Nazis?! They're all over the place. I'm getting out of here — *(Scar Tissue tries to leave. Marisol stops him.)*

MARISOL. Don't leave me!

SCAR TISSUE. Why? You're not alone, are you? You got your faith still intact. You still believe God is good. You still think you can glide through the world and not be part of it.

MARISOL. I'm not a Nazi!

SCAR TISSUE. I can't trust you. Ever since the angels went into open revolt, you can't trust your own mother ... oops. *(Marisol looks at him.)*

MARISOL. What did you say? You too? Did angels talk to you too?

SCAR TISSUE. *(Worried.)* No. Never mind. I don't know a thing. Just talking out my ass.

MARISOL. You didn't dream it —

SCAR TISSUE. *(Scared.)* I had enough punishment! I don't wanna get in the middle of some celestial Vietnam! I don't want any more angelic napalm dropped on me!

MARISOL. But I saw one too — I did — *what do all these visitations mean?* *(Marisol suddenly grabs Scar Tissue's hands — and he screams, pulls away, and cowers on the ground like a beaten dog.)*

SCAR TISSUE. NOT MY HANDS! Don't touch my hands! *(Scar*

Tissue rips his gloves off. His hands are covered in burn scars. He blows on his boiling hands.)

MARISOL. Oh my God.

SCAR TISSUE. *(Nearly crying.)* Heaven erupts but who pays the price? The fucking innocent do...!

MARISOL. What happened to you?

SCAR TISSUE. *(Crying.)* I was an air-traffic controller, Marisol Perez. I had a life. Then I saw angels in the radar screen and I started to drink. *(Marisol gets closer to the whimpering Scar Tissue. She has yet to really see his face. Marisol reaches out to him and pulls the hood back and removes his sunglasses. Scar Tissue's face has been horribly burned. She tries not to gasp, but she can't help it.)*

MARISOL. *Ay Dios, ay Dios mio, ay Dios ...*

SCAR TISSUE. You're looking for your friend ... everyone here is looking for something ... I'm looking for something too ...

MARISOL. What is it? Maybe I can help?

SCAR TISSUE. I'm looking for my lost skin. Have you seen my lost skin? It was once very pretty. We were very close. I was really attached to it. *(Scar Tissue runs to the trash bin and starts looking through it.)*

MARISOL. I haven't seen anything like that.

SCAR TISSUE. It's got to be somewhere ... it must be looking for me ... it must be lonely too, don't you think...?

MARISOL. Look, I'm sorry I bothered you, I'm, I'm going to go now ... *(Scar Tissue looks at Marisol.)*

SCAR TISSUE. I was just sleeping under the stars. It was another night when I couldn't find shelter. The places I went to, I got beat up. They took my clothes. Urinated in my mouth. Fucking blankets they gave me were laced with DDT. I said Fuck It, I took my shit outside and went up to some dickhead park in the Bronx ...

MARISOL. *(Remembering.)* Van Cortlandt Park?

SCAR TISSUE. ... just to be near some shriveled trees and alone and away from the massive noise, just for a little nap ... my eyes closed ... I vaguely remember the sound of goose-stepping teenagers from Staten Island with a can of gasoline, shouting orders in German ... *(Marisol walks away from Scar Tissue.)*

MARISOL. June's waiting for me ...

45

SCAR TISSUE. A flash of light. I exploded outward. My bubbling skin divorced my suffering nerves and ran away, looking for some coolness, some paradise, some other body to embrace! *(Laughs bitterly.)* Now I smell like barbecue! I could have eaten myself! I could have charged money for pieces of my broiled meat!

MARISOL. Please stop. I get the picture. *(Scar Tissue stops, looks at Marisol sadly. He motions to her that he needs help. She helps him with his gloves, sunglasses, hood.)*

SCAR TISSUE. The angel was Japanese. Dressed in armor. Dressed in iron. Dressed to endure the fire of war. She had a scimitar.

MARISOL. *(Can't believe it; wanting to.)* She?

SCAR TISSUE. Kissed me. I almost exploded. I kept hearing Jimi Hendrix in my middle ear as those lips, like two *brands*, nearly melted me. She was radiant. Raw.

MARISOL AND SCAR TISSUE. Fulgent.

SCAR TISSUE. She told me when angels are bored at night, they write your nightmares. She said the highest among the angels carry God's throne on their backs for eternity, singing, "Glory, glory, glory!" But her message was terrible and after she kissed me ...

MARISOL AND SCAR TISSUE. ... I spit at her.

SCAR TISSUE. Was that the right thing to do, Marisol?

MARISOL. I thought it was ... but I don't know. *(Marisol looks gently at Scar Tissue. She kisses him softly. He smiles and pats her on the head like a puppy. He goes to his wheelchair and pulls out an old bottle of Kentucky bourbon. He smiles and offers the bottle to Marisol. Marisol drinks greedily. Scar Tissue applauds her. She smiles as the hot liquid burns down her throat. She laughs long and loud: in this barren landscape, it's a beautiful sound. As they both laugh, Scar Tissue motions that they should embrace. Marisol holds her breath and embraces him.)*

SCAR TISSUE. *(Hopeful.)* So? Feelin' horny? Can I hope? *(Marisol quickly lets him go and gives him back his bottle.)*

MARISOL. Let's not push it, okay Elvis? *(Scar Tissue laughs. He goes to his wheelchair and prepares to hit the road again.)*

SCAR TISSUE. Word on the street is, water no longer seeks its own level, there are fourteen inches to the foot, six days in the week, seven planets in the solar system, and the French are polite. I also hear the sun rises in the north and sets in the south. I think I saw the sun setting over there ... instinct tells me south is over there ... *(Marisol turns to face south.)*

MARISOL. Thank you. *(The Skinhead crosses the stage again, with the can of gasoline, chasing the frightened Homeless Person. Marisol and Scar Tissue hit the ground. The Homeless Person falls. The Skinhead pours the gasoline on the Homeless Person and lights a match. There's a scream as the Homeless Person burns to death. Marisol covers her ears so she can't hear. The Skinhead exits. Marisol and Scar Tissue quickly get up. Marisol tries to run to the burnt Homeless Person. Scar Tissue stops her.)*

SCAR TISSUE. No! There's nothing you can do! Don't even look!

MARISOL. Oh my God ...

SCAR TISSUE. I gotta get outta here. Look — if you see some extra skin laying around somewhere ... pick it up for me, okay? I'll be exceedingly grateful. Bye. *(Scar Tissue gets back into his wheelchair.)*

MARISOL. Why don't we stay together — protect each other?

SCAR TISSUE. There is no protection. That Nazi is after me. He works for TRW. If I stay ... you're gonna have torturers and death squads all over you. *(Marisol goes toward him.)*

MARISOL. I'm not afraid —

SCAR TISSUE. No, I said! *Get away from me! Just get away from me!!* Are you fucking *CRAZY OR WHAT?* Just — just if you see my skin, beautiful ... have some good sex with it and tell it to come home quick. *(He's gone.)* I'll always love you, Marisol! *(Marisol is alone. More odd streaking lights rake the sky. Marisol hits the ground again, looking up, hoping that the barrage will end.)*

MARISOL. *(To herself.)* South — that way — I'll go south that way, where the sun sets, to look for June until I hit Miami — then — I'll know I passed her. *(The streaking lights stop. Marisol gets up. She takes a step. Then another step. With each step, the lights change as if she were entering a new part of the city or time has suddenly jumped forward. She finds some homeless person's old coat and puts it on.)* I'm getting dirty ... and my clothes smell bad ... I'm getting dirty and my clothes smell bad ... my fucking stomach's grumbling ... *(Marisol runs up to the metal trash bin. She ducks behind it. She takes a piss. She finishes and comes out from behind the trash bin, relieved. Grabbing her empty stomach, Marisol tries to think through her predicament. To the gold crown.)* Okay, I just wanna go home. I just wanna live with June — want my boring nine-to-five back — my two-weeks-out-of-the-year vacation — my intellectual detachment — my ability to read about the misery of the world and not lose a moment out of my busy day. To believe you really knew what you were doing, God — please — if the sun would just come *up! (Beat. To herself.)* But what if the sun doesn't come up? And this is it? It's the deadline. I'm against the wall. I'm at the rim of the apocalypse ... *(Marisol looks up. To the Angel.) Blessed guardian angel!* Maybe you were right. God has stopped looking. We can't live life as if nothing's changed. To live in the sweet past. To look backwards for our instructions. We have to reach up, beyond the debris, past the future, spit in the eye of the sun, make a fist, and say *no*, and say *no*, and say *no*, and say ... *(Beat. Doubts. To herself.)* ... no, what if she's wrong? *(She hurriedly gets on her knees to pray. Vicious, to the crown.)* Dear God, All-Powerful, All-Beautiful, what do I do now? How do I get out of this? Do I have to make a deal? Arrange payment and bail myself out? *What about it!?* I'll do anything! I'll spy for you. I'll steal for you. I'll decipher strange angelic codes and mine harbors and develop germ bombs and poison the angelic food supply. DEAR GOD, WHO DO I HAVE TO BETRAY TO GET OUT OF THIS FUCKING MESS?! *(It starts to snow lightly. Marisol can't believe it. She holds out her hand.)* Snow? It's eighty degrees! *(We hear the sound of bombs, heavy artillery, very close. Marisol is suddenly, violently, gripped by hunger pains. She grabs her stomach.)* Oh God! *(Marisol scrambles to the trash bin and starts burrowing into it like an animal searching for food. She finally finds a paper bag. She tears it open. She finds a bunch of moldy French fries. She closes her eyes and prepares to eat them.)*

LENNY'S VOICE.   Marisol you don't want to eat that! *(Marisol throws the food down.)*

MARISOL. *(To Herself.)* Lenny? *(Lenny comes in pushing a battered baby carriage full of junk. Lenny is nine months pregnant: huge belly, swollen breasts. Marisol is stunned by the transformation.)* Holy shit.

LENNY. Don't eat anything in that pile, Marisol. It's lethal.

MARISOL. — you're alive and you're ... bloated —

LENNY. Man who owned the restaurant on the other side of that wall put rat poison in the trash to discourage the homeless from picking through the pile. God bless the child that's got his own, huh? It's nice to see you again, Marisol. *(It stops snowing. Staring at his stomach, Marisol goes over to Lenny.)*

MARISOL. *(Amazed.)* I thought I killed you.

LENNY. Almost. But I forgive you. I forgive my sister, too.

MARISOL. You've seen her?

LENNY. I haven't seen her, sorry. Hey, you want food? I have a little food. I'll prepare you some secret edible food. *(Marisol goes to Lenny, wide-eyed.)*

MARISOL. Okay ... but ... Lenny ... you're immense ... *(Marisol helps Lenny sit. He motions for her to sit next to him.)*

LENNY. I'm fucking enormous. Got the worst hemorrhoids. The smell of Chinese food makes me puke my guts.

MARISOL. *(Embarrassed.)* I just don't know ... what to think about this ... and what would June say...?

LENNY. *(Chuckles.)* I have something you're gonna like, Marisol. Took me great pains to get. Lots of weaseling around the black market, greasing palms, you know, giving blow jobs — *the things a parent will do for their fetus!* — until I got it ... *(Lenny produces a bag. In the bag, Lenny reveals a scrawny little apple wrapped lovingly in layer after layer of delicate colored paper. Marisol can't believe what she sees.)*

MARISOL. That's an apple. But that's extinct.

LENNY. Only if you believe the networks. Powers-that-be got the very last tree. It's in the Pentagon. In the center of the five-sided beast. *(Lenny bites the apple, relishing its flavor. He pats his stomach approvingly. Marisol hungrily watches him eat.)* I was on a terrible diet 'til I got knocked up. Eating cigarette butts, old milk cartons, cat food, raw shoelaces, roach motels. It's nice to be able to give my baby a few essential vitamins.

MARISOL. You're really gonna be a mother?

LENNY. Baby's been kicking. It's got great aim. Always going for my bladder. I'm pissing every five minutes.

MARISOL. *(Tentative.)* Can I feel? *(Marisol puts her hand on Lenny's belly. She feels movement and pulls her hand away.)*

LENNY. It's impossible to sleep. Lying on my back, I'm crushed. On my side, I can't breathe. The baby's heartbeat keeps me up at night. The beating is dreadful. Sounds like a bomb. I know when it goes, it's gonna go BIG.

MARISOL. *(Frightened, unsure.)* Something's moving in there ...

LENNY. When it's in a good mood it does back flips and my fucking kidneys end up in my throat. Did I tell you about my hemorrhoids? Here, eat. *(Lenny gives Marisol the apple. She bites into it — chews — then quickly spits it all out. Livid, Lenny takes the apple away from Marisol.)* Don't waste my FOOD, *you dumb shit!* *(Lenny starts picking up the bits of half-chewed apple spit out by Marisol and eats them greedily. Marisol continues to spit.)*

MARISOL. *(Angry.)* It's just salt inside there ... just *salt* ...

LENNY. My baby's trying to build a brain! My baby needs all the minerals it can get!

MARISOL. It's not an apple! It's not food!

LENNY. Get outta here if you're gonna be ungrateful! My baby and I don't need you! *(Lenny devours the apple and tries to keep from crying.)* There isn't a single food group in the world that isn't pure salt anymore! Where the fuck have you been?! *(He holds his stomach for comfort.)*

MARISOL. This is your old bullshit, Lenny. That's a fucking pumpkin you got under your clothes. A big bundle of deceit and sexual CONFUSION. You're trying to *dislodge* me. Finally push me over the *edge*. Contradict *all* I know so I won't be able to say my own *name*. *(Marisol angrily pushes Lenny and he topples over, holding his stomach.)*

LENNY. There isn't much food left in the PENTAGON, you know!

MARISOL. Oh, give me a break. When the sun comes up in the morning, all this will be gone! The city will come back! People will go back to work. You'll be a myth. A folk tale. *(Bitter.)*

Maybe you should stop pretending you're pregnant and find a job.

LENNY. *How can you say that when this is your baby?!*

MARISOL. It's not my baby!

LENNY. For days and days all I did was think about you and think about you and the more I thought about you, the bigger I got! Of course it's yours!

MARISOL. I don't know what you're saying!

LENNY. I shouldda had a fucking *abortion* ...

MARISOL. *(Trying not to lose control.)* I think you're a freak, Lenny. I'm supposed to know that men don't have babies. But I don't know that anymore, do I? If you're really pregnant, then we have to start at the beginning, don't we? Well I'm not ready to do that! *(Lenny gets to his feet, indignant.)*

LENNY. I'm no freak. Every man should have this experience. There'd be fewer wars. *This* is power. *This* is energy. I guard my expanding womb greedily. I worship my new organs ... the violent bloodstream sending food and oxygen ... back and forth ... *between two hearts.* One body. Two surging hearts! *That's* a revolution! *(Lenny starts off. He stops in his tracks. He drops everything. He grabs his stomach. Pain knocks out his breathing.)*

MARISOL. Now what is it?

LENNY. Oh shit ... I think it's time. I think this is it.

MARISOL. Get outta here. *(Lenny's pants are suddenly wet.)*

LENNY. My water's burst. Oh God, it can't be now ...

MARISOL. I'm telling you to stop this!

LENNY. *(Panicking.)* I'm not ready. Feel my breasts! They're empty! I can't let this baby be born yet! What if my body can't make enough milk to feed my baby?! *(Lenny shrieks with pain, falls to his knees. Marisol helps him lie down. She kneels beside him.)*

MARISOL. Okay, Lenny, breathe — breathe — breathe —

LENNY. *(Incredible pain.)* I'm breathing, you ASSHOLE, I'm breathing!

MARISOL. Breathe more!

LENNY. Jesus, and I thought *war* was hell!

MARISOL. Oh my God — oh Jesus....

LENNY. If I pull off this birth thing, *it'll be a miracle!*

MARISOL. ... *Angel of God please help him! (Marisol quickly covers Lenny's abdomen with her coat. Lenny starts the final stage of labor. He bears down. Lenny lets out a final, cataclysmic scream. The baby is born. Marisol "catches" the baby. Marisol holds the silent baby in the coat, wrapping it tight. She examines the baby. Lenny's huge stomach has disappeared. He breathes hard. Short silence. Lenny sits up slowly, wiping sweat from his face, happy the ordeal is over. All Lenny wants to do is hold his child. Marisol stands up holding the baby, looking at it a long time, a troubled look on her face. Lenny holds out his arms for the baby. Marisol looks at Lenny and shakes her head, sadly, no. Lenny looks at Marisol, all hope drained from his face.)*

LENNY. Dead?

MARISOL. I'm sorry. *(Marisol wraps the baby tighter. Marisol gives Lenny his baby. Lenny takes the bundle, kisses it, holds back tears. Marisol looks at him.)*

LENNY. *(Grim.)* C'mon. There's something we have to do now. *(Holding the baby, Lenny starts to walk around and around the stage. Marisol follows. They come to the D. corner where the rosary-covered fire hydrant is. Special lighting on this area. Marisol looks down and notices little crucifixes scratched into the sidewalk in rows. Dazzling, frenetic lights rip the air above Marisol and Lenny.)* Do you know where you are, Marisol? *(Marisol shakes her head no.)* You're in Brooklyn.

MARISOL. *(Empty.)* Wow. I finally made it. I'm here.

LENNY. Everybody comes to this street eventually.

MARISOL. Why?

LENNY. People are buried here. It looks like a sidewalk. But it's not. It's a tomb.

MARISOL. For who?

LENNY. For babies. *Angelitos. (Lenny removes a slab of sidewalk concrete and starts digging up the dirt beneath it. There's a tiny wooden box there.)* The city provides these coffins. There are numbers on them. The city knows how we live. *(Lenny gently places the baby's body in the box.)* These are babies born on the street. Little girls of the twilight hours who never felt warm blankets around their bodies. Never drank their mothers' holy milk. Little boys born with coke in their blood. This is where babies who die on the street are taken to rest. You never heard of it?

MARISOL. Never. *(Lenny puts the box in the ground and covers it up with dirt.)*
LENNY. Everyone who sleeps and begs in the open air knows this address. We come with flowers, with crucifixes, with offerings. The wind plays organ music. Hard concrete turns into gentle moss so the babies can decompose in grace. We all come here sooner or later to pay respects to the most fragile of the street people. *(Lenny replaces the concrete slab and scratches the name of the child into the concrete. He says a prayer. If there are other Homeless People onstage, they pick up the prayer and repeat it softly underneath Lenny.)* Matthew, Mark, Luke, and John. Bless the bed that I lie on. Four corners to my bed. Four angels 'round my head. One to watch and one to pray. And two to bear your soul away. *(Lenny kisses the ground.)* 'Night, little Marisol. *(Lenny lies on the ground and falls asleep. Exhausted, Marisol looks at the tiny cemetery. She reads the names scratched into the sidewalk.)*
MARISOL. Fermin Rivera ... born March 14, died March 16 ... Jose Amengual ... born August 2, died August 2 ... Delfina Perez ... born December 23, died January 6 ... Jonathan Sand ... born July 1, died July 29 ... Wilfredo Terrón ... dates unknown ... no name ... no name ... no name ... *(Marisol can't read anymore. She sits in the middle of the child cemetery, exhausted, not able to think, feel or react anymore. For all she knows, this could be the end of the world. Marisol lies on the street, in Lenny's arms, and falls asleep. U. there's the sound of marching feet. The Skinhead enters and marches toward the sleeping Marisol and Lenny and stops. Only as the light comes up on the Skinhead do we realize it's June.)*
SKINHEAD. *(To herself, indicating Marisol.)* Look at this goddamn thing, this waste, this fucking parasite. God, I'm so sick of it. Sick of the eyesore. Sick of the diseases. Sick of the drugs. Sick of the homelessness. Sick of the border babies. Sick of the dark skin. Sick of that compassion thing! That's where it all started! When they put in that fucking compassion thing! *(Furious.)* I mean, why can't they just go AWAY? I mean, okay, if you people want to kill yourselves, fine, do it: kill yourselves with your crack and your incest and your promiscuity and your homo anal intercourse ... just leave me to take care of myself and my own. Leave

me to my gardens. I'm good in my gardens. I'm good on my acres of green grass. God distributes green grass in just the right way! Take care of your own. Take care of your family. If everybody did that ... I swear on my gold Citibank MasterCard ... there wouldn't be any problems, anywhere, in the next millennium ... *(June looks down at Marisol. She unscrews the can of gasoline and starts pouring gasoline on Marisol and Lenny. Marisol wakes up. June strikes a match. Marisol jumps at June, grabbing her.)*

MARISOL.   Cut that shit out you fucking Nazi! *(June tries to throw the match on Marisol.)*

JUNE.   Stay still so I can burn you! *(Marisol grabs June and tries to push her away from Lenny. They're face to face for the first time.)* What a day I'm having, huh?

MARISOL.   *(Startled.)* ... June?

JUNE.   I started out burning hobos and ended up torching half the city! The entire Upper West Side up in ashes!

MARISOL.   *(Overjoyed.)* Oh God, I found you.

JUNE.   You got anything for me?!

MARISOL.   I thought Lenny killed you —

JUNE.   You got nothing for me? Get outta my way, asshole!

MARISOL.   Don't you remember me?

JUNE.   You should see what I did! It's fire on a massive scale! Buildings melted all down! Consumed! Ashes of those evaporated dreams are all over the fucking place!

MARISOL.   June — it's Marisol.... *(Marisol throws both arms around June, embraces her tightly, and kisses her. June tries to escape.)*

JUNE.   We could be picked up real fast by the police ... they've built great big facilities for us ... 'cause our numbers are swelling ... *(Marisol tries to hold June. June resists. But the prolonged and violent contact with Marisol's body has started to awaken June's memory. She begins to sound a little like her old self.)* But they won't take me! I have a strategy now! I burn bag people! The troop likes that!

MARISOL.   No more! That's not you! *(Marisol throws the can of gasoline into the trash bin. She grabs June's hand and pulls June toward Lenny. June resists.)*

JUNE.   The Citicorps building was a great place to hide. A man would pull your teeth for free in Port Authority —

MARISOL.   Lenny's right here ...

JUNE.   I hear the water in the Central Park reservoir is salty 'cause angels are falling outta the sky, Marisol ...

MARISOL.   *(Astonished.)* You said my name. You said Marisol. *(Marisol joyfully embraces June and kisses her. That pushes June over the edge, and she collapses. Marisol catches her and lays her gently on the ground. Marisol sits with June's head on her lap. This time June does not resist.)*

JUNE.   *(Weak, rubbing her head.)* I can't understand these nightmares I'm having ... *(Marisol holds June. June and Lenny quietly start to cry.)*

MARISOL.   We survived. We survived, June. *(Marisol looks around her — at her two crippled, sobbing friends — at the distorted world — all too aware of the graveyard which has become the site of their reunion.)* For what? To do what? *(Marisol looks up at the crown — a long, still moment.)* Fuck you. Just *fuck you!* *(Loud machine-gun fire rips the air. Marisol hits the ground and covers June and Lenny with her body.)* June, Lenny ... don't you guys worry ... I have a clear vision for us. I know what I want to do. *(The machine-gun firing stops. Marisol kisses her friends.)* Listen to me. We're going to find the angels. And I'm going to ask them to touch your foreheads. To press their angelic fingers into your temples. Fire your minds with instant light. Blow up your bad dreams. And resurrect you. *(Marisol looks up at the crown.)* And then we're going to join them. Then we're going to fight with the angels. *(Marisol helps June and Lenny to their feet. June and Lenny see each other and embrace.)*

LENNY.   *(To June.)* I'm sorry for everything I did ...

JUNE.   *(To Lenny, kissing him.)* I'm sorry, too, Lenny ... *(As Marisol takes their hands to start their new journey, the Woman With Furs enters, unseen, behind them. She is completely still. She is holding an Uzi.)*

MARISOL.   What a time to be alive, huh? On one hand, we're nothing. We're dirt. On the other hand, we're the reason the universe was made. *(The Woman With Furs loads the Uzi. Bombs are heard.)*

JUNE. What's that noise?

MARISOL. Right now, thousands upon millions of angels are dying on our behalf. Isn't that amazing? The silver cities of Heaven are burning for us. Attacks and counterattacks are ruining galaxies. The ripped-up planets are making travel impossible. And triumphant angels are taking over the television stations. All for us. All for me. *(The Woman With Furs points the Uzi at Marisol, June and Lenny.)*

WOMAN WITH FURS. Sorry, Marisol. We don't need revolution here. We can't have upheaval at the drop of a hat. No demonstrations here! No putting up pamphlets! No shoving daisies into the rifles of militiamen! No stopping tanks by standing in their way! *(Marisol turns to look at the Woman With Furs.)*

MARISOL. ... Unless you want to join us — ?

WOMAN WITH FURS. Traitors! Credit risks! *(Marisol goes to the Woman With Furs, and the Woman With Furs blasts Marisol, pumping hundreds of rounds into her. She dies instantly and falls to the ground. The Woman With Furs exits. There's a blackout. Suddenly, the stage is bathed in strange light. We hear the strange, indecipherable sounds of the angelic war. June and Lenny kneel where Marisol has fallen. Marisol is standing apart, alone, in her own light. Marisol's voice is slightly amplified.)*

MARISOL. I'm killed instantly. Little blazing lead meteors enter my body. My blood cells ride those bullets into outer space. My soul surges up the oceans of the Milky Way at the speed of light. At the moment of death, I see the invisible war. *(Beautiful music. The stage goes black, except for a light on Marisol.)* Thousands of years of fighting pass in an instant. New and terrible forms of warfare, monstrous weapons and unimagined strains of terror are created and destroyed in billionths of a second. Galaxies spring from a single drop of angel's sweat while hundreds of armies fight and die on the fingertips of children in the Bronx. *(Light U. reveals the Angel. She's dressed in a filthy, tattered uniform: the war has ravaged her. She also has huge magnificent wings: her wings of war. She's got an Uzi machine gun. The Angel fires her Uzi into the air, at the invisible legions of God's loyal warriors. The terrible sounds of war. The angelic vision lasts only seconds. The stage once again goes to black. A spotlight on Marisol.)* Three hundred million million beautiful angels die in the first charge of the Final Battle. The oceans are salty with rebel blood. Angels drop like lightning from the dying sky. The rebels are in full retreat. There's chaos. There's blood and fire and ambulances and Heaven's soldiers scream and fight and die in beautiful, beautiful light. It looks like the revolution is doomed ... *(Light U. reveals a single Homeless Person angrily throwing rocks at the sky. The Homeless Person is joined by Lenny and June. This vision lasts only seconds. The stage once again goes to black. A spotlight on Marisol.)* ... then, as if one body, one mind, the innocent of the earth take to the streets with anything they can find — rocks, sticks, screams — and aim their displeasure at the senile sky and fire into the tattered wind on the side of the angels ... billions of poor, of homeless, of peaceful, of silent, of angry ... fighting and fighting as no species has ever fought before. Inspired by the earthly noise, the rebels advance! *(A small moon appears in the sky, far, far away.)* New ideas rip the Heavens. New powers are created. New miracles are signed into law. It's the first day of the new history ... *(There's a few seconds of tremendous noise as the war hits its climax. Then silence. The Angel appears next to Marisol, wingless, unarmed, holding the gold crown in her hands. The Angel holds the crown out to the audience as Marisol looks at her.)* Oh God. What light. What possibilities. What hope. *(The Angel kisses Marisol. Bright, bright light begins to shine directly into the audience's eyes — for several seconds — and Marisol, the Angel, June, Lenny and the Homeless People seem to be turned into light. Then all seem to disappear in the wild light of the new millennium — quick blackout.)*

END OF PLAY

PROPERTY LIST

The New York *Times* (MARISOL)
Golf club (MAN WITH GOLF CLUB)
Pillow (MARISOL)
Knife (MARISOL)
Drink (MARISOL)
Crucifix (MARISOL)
Horseshoe (MARISOL)
Rabbit's foot (MARISOL)
Prayer cards (MARISOL)
Milagros (MARISOL)
Medicine bundles (MARISOL)
Statuettes of Buddha (MARISOL)
Other good-luck charms (MARISOL)
Shoe (MARISOL)
Pile of salt (MARISOL)
The New York *Post* (JUNE)
Radio (JUNE)
Manuscript (MARISOL)
Ice cream cone (MAN WITH ICE CREAM)
Phone (JUNE)
Uzi submachine gun (ANGEL, WOMAN WITH FURS)
Coat (JUNE)
Sculpture of nails (LENNY)
Stacks of homemade magazines (LENNY)
Homemade guitars (LENNY)
Kitchen knife (LENNY)
Coat (LENNY)
Bag of golf clubs (LENNY)
Money (JUNE)
Keys (JUNE)
Wildflowers (LENNY)
Silver wings (ANGEL)
Golf club (MARISOL)
Newspaper (WOMAN WITH FURS)
Magnet (MAN WITH SCAR TISSUE)

Magazines and newspapers (MAN WITH SCAR TISSUE)
The New York *Post* (MAN WITH SCAR TISSUE)
Can of gasoline (SKINHEAD)
Bottle of bourbon (MAN WITH SCAR TISSUE)
Match (SKINHEAD)
Old coat (MARISOL)
Paper bag containing moldy French fries (MARISOL)
Baby carriage full of junk (LENNY)
Bag containing apple (LENNY)
Baby (MARISOL)
Tiny wooden coffin (LENNY)
Rocks (HOMELESS PERSON, LENNY, JUNE)
Gold crown (ANGEL)

SOUND EFFECTS

Noises of Marisol's apartment building: doors slamming, bottles
    smashing, radiator pipes pounding, stereos playing, etc.
Sound of gun being cocked
Crickets
Distant explosions
Distant thunder and lightning
Alarm clock
Radio voice
Distant rumblings
Bombs, heavy artillery
Machine-gun fire
Bombs
Sounds of the angelic war
Beautiful music

NEW PLAYS

★ **GUARDIANS by Peter Morris.** In this unflinching look at war, a disgraced American soldier discloses the truth about Abu Ghraib prison, and a clever English journalist reveals how he faked a similar story for the London tabloids. "Compelling, sympathetic and powerful." *–NY Times.* "Sends you into a state of moral turbulence." *–Sunday Times (UK).* "Nothing short of remarkable." *–Village Voice.* [1M, 1W] ISBN: 978-0-8222-2177-7

★ **BLUE DOOR by Tanya Barfield.** Three generations of men (all played by one actor), from slavery through Black Power, challenge Lewis, a tenured professor of mathematics, to embark on a journey combining past and present. "A teasing flare for words." *–Village Voice.* "Unfailingly thought-provoking." *–LA Times.* "The play moves with the speed and logic of a dream." *–Seattle Weekly.* [2M] ISBN: 978-0-8222-2209-5

★ **THE INTELLIGENT DESIGN OF JENNY CHOW by Rolin Jones.** This irreverent "techno-comedy" chronicles one brilliant woman's quest to determine her heritage and face her fears with the help of her astounding creation called Jenny Chow. "Boldly imagined." *–NY Times.* "Fantastical and funny." *–Variety.* "Harvests many laughs and finally a few tears." *–LA Times.* [3M, 3W] ISBN: 978-0-8222-2071-8

★ **SOUVENIR by Stephen Temperley.** Florence Foster Jenkins, a wealthy society eccentric, suffers under the delusion that she is a great coloratura soprano—when in fact the opposite is true. "Hilarious and deeply touching. Incredibly moving and breathtaking." *–NY Daily News.* "A sweet love letter of a play." *–NY Times.* "Wildly funny. Completely charming." *–Star-Ledger.* [1M, 1W] ISBN: 978-0-8222-2157-9

★ **ICE GLEN by Joan Ackermann.** In this touching period comedy, a beautiful poetess dwells in idyllic obscurity on a Berkshire estate with a band of unlikely cohorts. "A beautifully written story of nature and change." *–Talkin' Broadway.* "A lovely play which will leave you with a lot to think about." *–CurtainUp.* "Funny, moving and witty." *–Metroland (Boston).* [4M, 3W] ISBN: 978-0-8222-2175-3

★ **THE LAST DAYS OF JUDAS ISCARIOT by Stephen Adly Guirgis.** Set in a time-bending, darkly comic world between heaven and hell, this play reexamines the plight and fate of the New Testament's most infamous sinner. "An unforced eloquence that finds the poetry in lowdown street talk." *–NY Times.* "A real jaw-dropper." *–Variety.* "An extraordinary play." *–Guardian (UK).* [10M, 5W] ISBN: 978-0-8222-2082-4

DRAMATISTS PLAY SERVICE, INC.
440 Park Avenue South, New York, NY 10016 212-683-8960 Fax 212-213-1539
postmaster@dramatists.com   www.dramatists.com

NEW PLAYS

★ **THE GREAT AMERICAN TRAILER PARK MUSICAL music and lyrics by David Nehls, book by Betsy Kelso.** Pippi, a stripper on the run, has just moved into Armadillo Acres, wreaking havoc among the tenants of Florida's most exclusive trailer park. "Adultery, strippers, murderous ex-boyfriends, Costco and the Ice Capades. Undeniable fun." *–NY Post.* "Joyful and unashamedly vulgar." *–The New Yorker.* "Sparkles with treasure." *–New York Sun.* [2M, 5W] ISBN: 978-0-8222-2137-1

★ **MATCH by Stephen Belber.** When a young Seattle couple meet a prominent New York choreographer, they are led on a fraught journey that will change their lives forever. "Uproariously funny, deeply moving, enthralling theatre." *–NY Daily News.* "Prolific laughs and ear-to-ear smiles." *–NY Magazine.* [2M, 1W] ISBN: 978-0-8222-2020-6

★ **MR. MARMALADE by Noah Haidle.** Four-year-old Lucy's imaginary friend, Mr. Marmalade, doesn't have much time for her—not to mention he has a cocaine addiction and a penchant for pornography. "Alternately hilarious and heartbreaking." *–The New Yorker.* "A mature and accomplished play." *–LA Times.* "Scathingly observant comedy." *–Miami Herald.* [4M, 2W] ISBN: 978-0-8222-2142-5

★ **MOONLIGHT AND MAGNOLIAS by Ron Hutchinson.** Three men cloister themselves as they work tirelessly to reshape a screenplay that's just not working—*Gone with the Wind.* "Consumers of vintage Hollywood insider stories will eat up Hutchinson's diverting conjecture." *–Variety.* "A lot of fun." *–NY Post.* "A Hollywood dream-factory farce." *–Chicago Sun-Times.* [3M, 1W] ISBN: 978-0-8222-2084-8

★ **THE LEARNED LADIES OF PARK AVENUE by David Grimm, translated and freely adapted from Molière's *Les Femmes Savantes*.** Dicky wants to marry Betty, but her mother's plan is for Betty to wed a most pompous man. "A brave, brainy and barmy revision." *–Hartford Courant.* "A rare but welcome bird in contemporary theatre." *–New Haven Register.* "Roll over Cole Porter." *–Boston Globe.* [5M, 5W] ISBN: 978-0-8222-2135-7

★ **REGRETS ONLY by Paul Rudnick.** A sparkling comedy of Manhattan manners that explores the latest topics in marriage, friendships and squandered riches. "One of the funniest quip-meisters on the planet." *–NY Times.* "Precious moments of hilarity. Devastatingly accurate political and social satire." *–BackStage.* "Great fun." *–CurtainUp.* [3M, 3W] ISBN: 978-0-8222-2223-1

DRAMATISTS PLAY SERVICE, INC.
440 Park Avenue South, New York, NY 10016   212-683-8960   Fax 212-213-1539
postmaster@dramatists.com   www.dramatists.com

NEW PLAYS

★ **AFTER ASHLEY by Gina Gionfriddo.** A teenager is unwillingly thrust into the national spotlight when a family tragedy becomes talk-show fodder. "A work that virtually any audience would find accessible." —*NY Times.* "Deft character-ization and caustic humor." —*NY Sun.* "A smart satirical drama." —*Variety.* [4M, 2W] ISBN: 978-0-8222-2099-2

★ **THE RUBY SUNRISE by Rinne Groff.** Twenty-five years after Ruby struggles to realize her dream of inventing the first television, her daughter faces similar battles of faith as she works to get Ruby's story told on network TV. "Measured and intelligent, optimistic yet clear-eyed." —*NY Magazine.* "Maintains an exciting sense of ingenuity." —*Village Voice.* "Sinuous theatrical flair." —*Broadway.com.* [3M, 4W] ISBN: 978-0-8222-2140-1

★ **MY NAME IS RACHEL CORRIE taken from the writings of Rachel Corrie, edited by Alan Rickman and Katharine Viner.** This solo piece tells the story of Rachel Corrie who was killed in Gaza by an Israeli bulldozer set to demol-ish a Palestinian home. "Heartbreaking urgency. An invigoratingly detailed por-trait of a passionate idealist." —*NY Times.* "Deeply authentically human." —*USA Today.* "A stunning dramatization." —*CurtainUp.* [1W] ISBN: 978-0-8222-2222-4

★ **ALMOST, MAINE by John Cariani.** A cast of Mainers (or "Mainiacs" if you prefer) fall in and out of love in ways that only people who live in close proximity to wild moose can do. "A whimsical approach to the joys and perils of romance." —*NY Times.* "Sweet, poignant and witty." —*NY Daily News.* "John Cariani aims for the heart by way of the funny bone." —*Star-Ledger.* [2M, 2W] ISBN: 978-0-8222-2156-2

★ **Mitch Albom's TUESDAYS WITH MORRIE by Jeffrey Hatcher and Mitch Albom, based on the book by Mitch Albom.** The true story of Brandeis University professor Morrie Schwartz and his relationship with his stu-dent Mitch Albom. "A touching, life-affirming, deeply emotional drama." —*NY Daily News.* "You'll laugh. You'll cry." —*Variety.* "Moving and powerful." —*NY Post.* [2M] ISBN: 978-0-8222-2188-3

★ **DOG SEES GOD: CONFESSIONS OF A TEENAGE BLOCKHEAD by Bert V. Royal.** An abused pianist and a pyromaniac ex-girlfriend contribute to the teen-angst of America's most hapless kid. "A welcome antidote to the notion that the *Peanuts* gang provides merely American cuteness." —*NY Times.* "Hysterically funny." —*NY Post.* "The *Peanuts* kids have finally come out of their shells." —*Time Out.* [4M, 4W] ISBN: 978-0-8222-2152-4

DRAMATISTS PLAY SERVICE, INC.
440 Park Avenue South, New York, NY 10016 212-683-8960 Fax 212-213-1539
postmaster@dramatists.com **www.dramatists.com**

NEW PLAYS

★ **RABBIT HOLE by David Lindsay-Abaire.** Winner of the 2007 Pulitzer Prize. Becca and Howie Corbett have everything a couple could want until a life-shattering accident turns their world upside down. "An intensely emotional examination of grief, laced with wit." –*Variety.* "A transcendent and deeply affecting new play." –*Entertainment Weekly.* "Painstakingly beautiful." –*BackStage.* [2M, 3W] ISBN: 978-0-8222-2154-8

★ **DOUBT, A Parable by John Patrick Shanley.** Winner of the 2005 Pulitzer Prize and Tony Award. Sister Aloysius, a Bronx school principal, takes matters into her own hands when she suspects the young Father Flynn of improper relations with one of the male students. "All the elements come invigoratingly together like clockwork." –*Variety.* "Passionate, exquisite, important, engrossing." –*NY Newsday.* [1M, 3W] ISBN: 978-0-8222-2219-4

★ **THE PILLOWMAN by Martin McDonagh.** In an unnamed totalitarian state, an author of horrific children's stories discovers that someone has been making his stories come true. "A blindingly bright black comedy." –*NY Times.* "McDonagh's least forgiving, bravest play." –*Variety.* "Thoroughly startling and genuinely intimidating." –*Chicago Tribune.* [4M, 5 bit parts (2M, 1W, 1 boy, 1 girl)] ISBN: 978-0-8222-2100-5

★ **GREY GARDENS book by Doug Wright, music by Scott Frankel, lyrics by Michael Korie.** The hilarious and heartbreaking story of Big Edie and Little Edie Bouvier Beale, the eccentric aunt and cousin of Jacqueline Kennedy Onassis, once bright names on the social register who became East Hampton's most notorious recluses. "An experience no passionate theatergoer should miss." –*NY Times.* "A unique and unmissable musical." –*Rolling Stone.* [4M, 3W, 2 girls] ISBN: 978-0-8222-2181-4

★ **THE LITTLE DOG LAUGHED by Douglas Carter Beane.** Mitchell Green could make it big as the hot new leading man in Hollywood if Diane, his agent, could just keep him in the closet. "Devastatingly funny." –*NY Times.* "An out-and-out delight." –*NY Daily News.* "Full of wit and wisdom." –*NY Post.* [2M, 2W] ISBN: 978-0-8222-2226-2

★ **SHINING CITY by Conor McPherson.** A guilt-ridden man reaches out to a therapist after seeing the ghost of his recently deceased wife. "Haunting, inspired and glorious." –*NY Times.* "Simply breathtaking and astonishing." –*Time Out.* "A thoughtful, artful, absorbing new drama." –*Star-Ledger.* [3M, 1W] ISBN: 978-0-8222-2187-6

DRAMATISTS PLAY SERVICE, INC.
440 Park Avenue South, New York, NY 10016 212-683-8960 Fax 212-213-1539
postmaster@dramatists.com www.dramatists.com